PASCAL'S WAGER

Pascal's Wager

A Study of Practical Reasoning in Philosophical Theology

NICHOLAS RESCHER

University of Notre Dame Press
Notre Dame, Indiana 46556

Library of Congress Cataloging in Publication Data

Rescher, Nicholas.
Pascal's wager.

Includes bibliographical references and index.
1. God—Proof. 2. Philosophical theology—Methodology. 3. Risk-taking (Psychology) 4. Faith. 5. God—Knowableness. 6. Pascal, Blaise, 1623–1662. Pensées.
I. Title.
BT102.R38 1985 212'.1 84-40820
ISBN 0-268-01556-2

Manufactured in the United States of America

William Clancy

in memoriam

Contents

Preface

This little book is emphatically not an exercise in Pascal scholarship or exegesis; its main task is the *philosophical scrutiny of the line of thought that he pursued.* The historical description of Pascal's particular dealings with the relevant ideas is subordinated to this end. The book is thus concerned primarily with these issues of philosophical theology themselves, rather than with their role in the concrete historical setting of Pascal's own thought and writing.

The idea of the book arose in my mind in the spring of 1981. I was then writing *Risk* (Washington, D.C.: University Press of America, 1983), and was led to reflect on Pascal's Wager argument in this connection. But the project itself had to be squeezed into the interstices of other work. It was drafted in Oxford during the summer of 1981, reworked there during the summer of 1982, and polished during the summer of 1983. It was genuinely a sideshow—the product of vacation times in that home of lost causes.

The book has four chapters. The first examines the details of Pascal's Wager argument. The second deals, generally and abstractly, with the epistemological issues posed by the pragmatic route to the validation of beliefs. The third proceeds in the spirit of Pascal to look at some arguments of philosophical theology from the vantage point afforded by modern decision theory. Finally, the concluding chapter considers whether this sort of practicalistic, interest-oriented argumentation has any useful place at all in theological deliberations. The overall aim of the discussion is to show that Pascal's notorious Wager argument was the vehicle of a fruitful and valuable insight—one which not only represents a milestone in the development of an historically important tradition of thought but can still be seen as making an instructive contribution to philosophical theology.

Pascal's *Thoughts* (*Pensées*), of which the Wager argument passage is a minute part, is a collection of jottings that was unpublished in his own day. It was originally published by its Port Royal editors only eight years after Pascal's death in 1670, although a summary of the argument had already been presented at the end of the Port Royal *Logic* (1662). Many modern versions are available. The indefatigable Pascal scholar Louis Lafuma alone produced five editions. Four were based on the order of Pascal's collected material as his literary executors had them copied (in duplicate) for preservation and later editing (the "Copy").[1] Lafuma also issued a rationalized version of the text in which all the fragments are classified either under one of Pascal's own topical headings or in various appendices (Paris: Delmas, 1952). It is in this numerical ordering that the *Pensées* are cited here, cross-referenced to the older authoritative edition of Léon Brunschvicg (Paris: Hachette, 1914).

An English translation of the *Pensées* by John Warrington, based on Lafuma's Delmas edition, is included in the Everyman's Library series (London and New York, 1960); and the English quotations cited here are based on Warrington's translation. An excellent rendering by A. J. Krailsheimer, in the arrangement of the "Copy" as per the other Lafuma editions, has been issued by Penguin Books (Harmondsworth and Baltimore, 1966).

I am grateful to Linda Butera (who saw the book through many typescript revisions), to Richard Gale (who discussed the project with me and let me try out some of the ideas while guest lecturer in his philosophy of religion course at the University of Pittsburgh), and to Timo Airaksinen and Bryson Brown (who read the book in typescript and made useful suggestions for its improvement), and James Allis (who helped to correct the proofs).

Oxford
Summer, 1983

I
Pascal's Turning

1. Background of the Wager Argument

Pascal's *Thoughts* (*Pensées*) is a large assemblage of brief notes and drafts that he jotted down during the years 1657–62 in preparation for writing a projected *Apology for the Christian Religion.* The passage which concerns us is a minuscule part of this whole. It consists of two leaves, covered on both sides by handwriting overlapping in several directions, full of erasures and emendations.[2] This brief text endeavors to present a new line of thought in support of Christian religious faith. Pascal himself was deeply persuaded of the importance and novelty of these deliberations. Toward the end of the text, which takes the form of a dialogue between him and an unbelieving friend, his interlocutor exclaims: "Oh, your discourse delights me, carries me away!" However, to judge by the tenor of the large literature to which this small passage has given rise, Pascal's imaginary friend is very much in the minority in this regard.

Pascal's Wager argument can hardly be said to have set the world on fire. From its inception to the present day, when philosophers and theologians deign to mention it at all, they tend to do so by way of scornful dismissal. It is no exaggeration to say, with one nineteenth-century student of Pascal, that the argument "has been a scandal even to some of his greatest admirers."[3] Theologians have treated it with lofty disdain, and "philosophers feel it somehow as a professional obligation not to accept its cogency."[4]

And yet, as this brief book will try to show, the charges of moral insensitivity and other such high-minded complaints often launched against the argument are based on a total misunderstanding of its aim and import, and reflect a callous refusal to accept the argument on its own terms. Only by failing to recognize the job that Pascal's argument is designed to accomplish—by seeing it as attempting a task altogether different from its actual probative aim—can one support the facile recriminations all too often thrown its way. And this is hardly reasonable: surely any argument can be made to look silly if reconstrued to aim at conclusions never even remotely intended for it.

In actual fact, Pascal's Wager argument contains the core of a deeply insightful innovation. Its ground-breaking idea of a theological use of practical reason marks an important departure which, in the hands of such subsequent masters as Immanuel Kant and William James, has come to make a substantial impact on the philosophy of religion.

*****

The Wager argument passage opens with the following prologue:

> *Infini-rien*; infinity-nothing. Our soul has been cast into the body, where it finds number, time, dimension. Thereupon it reasons and calls this nature or necessity, and can believe nothing else. Yet unity added to infinity adds nothing to it, any more than one foot added to an infinite length. The finite is annihilated in presence of the infinite, and becomes pure nothingness. Even thus does our intellect stand to God. (*Pensées*, 343/233)

The close connection with Descartes' Fourth Meditation is striking:

> I am a kind of intermediate between God and nothingness, between the Supreme Being and non-being (*non ens*). My nature is such that, in so far as I am a creature of the Supreme Being, I have nothing in me to deceive me or lead me astray. Yet in so far as I also participate somehow in nothingness, non-being—that is, in so far as I am not myself the Supreme Being, and am lacking in no end of things—it is not surprising that I am deceived.[5]

To be sure, Pascal himself will hear nothing of intermediation: in relation to God, man stands squarely on the side of nothingness. But the similarities outweigh the differences. Descartes and Pascal alike see man's inadequacy as paramount. Both stress man's utter dependency on God for whatever goods he may enjoy—cognitive goods prominently included. The matter of justification in the face of skeptical doubts is part of the common problem-heritage of these thinkers. And the starting point of Pascal's Wager is clearly Descartes: its drama is played out on the stage of Cartesian skepticism.

Moreover, the strategy of Pascal's Wager argument in philosophical theology can fruitfully be viewed against the background of the Cartesian revolution in philosophy. Descartes put man as knower at the center of the stage. Instead of addressing questions regarding the nature of reality *directly,* the issue of our *knowledge* became the pivot point. Beginning with the question *How do I really know?,* Descartes assigned to God the pivotal role of guarantor of our knowledge of the world. And he maintained that man can come to know about the existence and nature of God through the light of God-given reason alone. God, our maker, has implanted an idea of himself in our minds somewhat as a silversmith impresses his hallmark into his product. This idea provides the basis on which we humans, relying wholly on our innate intellectual resources, can come to knowledge of God's nature and existence through the clear and distinct intuitions of our mind in much the same way that we come to know the truths of mathematics and metaphysics. As far as the mechanism of our knowledge is concerned, the necessity of God is, for Descartes, on the same cognitive plane as the necessity of the Pythagorean theorem or that of the non-vacuity of space.

Pascal retained Descartes's skeptically inspired preoccupation with the processes and products of the human intellect. But he abandoned Descartes' reliance on cognitive operations of human reason, and thus his orientation toward demonstrative knowledge. "The metaphysical proofs of God are so remote from human reasoning, and so complicated, that they make little impression. If some find them profitable, it is only at the moment when they grasp them; an hour later they fear they have been mistaken."[6] In place of Descartes's Thomistic/scholastic concern for demonstrating the existence of God, Pascal substitutes an Augustinian concern for the validation of *belief* in a God who is beyond the reach of the unaided human intellect and outside the grasp of feeble human reason. Indeed, knowledge as such would not really serve our needs in this domain: "There is a great difference between the knowledge and the love of God."[7] God lies beyond the reach of our ordinary cognitive resources: "If there is a God, he is infinitely incomprehensible, since, having neither parts nor limits, He has no affinity to us. We are incapable of knowing either what He is or if He is. God is *deus absconditus, Dieu caché,* a hidden God."[8]

As Pascal sees it, reasoning can only impel the outsider into the fold of believers by a circuitous route: what we can establish by reasoning is not the direct conclusion that there is a God, but only that oblique result that *belief* in God is warranted. The task is not to deploy the processes of rational demonstration to "prove" to skeptical outsiders that God exists (in Pascal's opinion a hopeless endeavor—as the skeptics have established), but to show uncommitted indifferentists that *belief* in God is rationally legitimate. Pascal holds, with the Renaissance skeptics, that our human resources for securing knowledge by inquiring reason are wholly inadequate to the demands of apologetics. For Pascal the pivotal question is thus no longer *How can one demonstrate that a God of such-and-such a character exists?* but rather, *How can one validate having faith in such a God?* He writes:

> It is a remarkable fact that none of the canonical writers ever employed nature to prove God. They all endeavor to instil belief in him. David, Solomon, and the rest never said: "There is no void, therefore there is a God." They must have had more knowledge than the most learned men who came after them, all of whom used such an argument. This is highly significant. (*Pensées*, 19/243)

Pascal shifts the issue from the demonstration of facts to the justification of faith. And he presses this question in the face of a profound skepticism regarding the capacity of reason in the theological sphere—one deeper than that of Descartes. Pascal turns to faith rather than theoretical reason precisely because of substantial doubts regarding the capabilities of the latter.

The pivotal issue with respect to belief is not one of rational *feasibility* alone; *desirability* also enters in. Would we really rest content with a God whose existence is a matter of demonstration? Is the God who emerges at the end of a syllogism (or some yet more complex course of demonstration) the sort of God we need or want? Pascal thinks not. He anticipates Kierkegaard's view that insufficiency in point of proof and evidence is advantageous, indeed even necessary to a viable faith.

Accordingly, a transposition is at issue here that might be called "Pascal's shift in theological argumentation"—a shift away from *theoretical* arguments that purport to argue probatively for the existence of God (in the manner of Aquinas' five ways) to a different style of *practical* argumentation, geared not to a theoretical demonstration of the existence of God as an ontological fact but to a practical resolution regarding what we ought to believe. The salient feature of the argument is thus its recourse to praxis—and to prudence.

Notwithstanding its methodological modernity as a course of argumentation cast in the mold of decision theory, the spirit of Pascal's Wager is thus profoundly conservative in its substantive message. It turns its back on a medieval scholasticism that had left its deep marks as recently as Descartes's unacknowledged borrowings from Suarez and returns to the perspectives of the Church Fathers. Its noncognitivism, its practicalism/voluntarism, and its Augustinian fideism are all throwbacks to an earlier era of Christian religious thought.

Yet despite its backward-looking aspect, the approach taken by Pascal breaks significant new ground in philosophical theology. Renaissance Christian skeptics from Nicholas of Cusa to Erasmus had emphasized the inadequacy of human reason in theological matters and urged the sufficiency of simple *piety* in religious practice unsupported by any warrant from doctrines and dogmas—i.e., without the rationalization of a justificatory basis of accepted theses. Luther had rejected such a noncognitivist approach as unworthy of a rational creature, holding that piety without rational conviction is not just rationally unsatisfying but even hypocritical. Pascal sought for a middle way between Erasmus' corrosive skepticism regarding reason and Luther's dogmatic insistence on the evidential legitimacy of belief through scripture and reason. In Montaigne, who greatly influenced Pascal, we are offered a stark choice between a religion based on cognitive reason and evidence and one resting on faith alone, based not on our capacities but solely on God's grace.[9] Pascal sought to find an intermediate route via the mitigated skepticism of the Middle Academy by arguing that belief can be validated on other than strictly evidential grounds, namely, on grounds of *practical* reason—as an instrumentality of action rather than theoretical cognition. As he saw it, considerations of praxis geared to the interest of man can provide the crucial linking *tertium quid* between the two problematic extremes of skepticism and dogmatism.

Pascal's shift away from the rational conviction secured by demonstrative reason has important consequences. To accept something, to believe in something, and to place one's trust in something can all be seen as *actions* of a certain sort, things that one can decide on and do, or else decide against and refrain from. Accordingly, the level of the discussion is shifted from *establishing a fact* to *justifying an action.* Such a shift from the cognitive (or theoretical) to the practical use of human reasoning puts the discussion on an entirely different basis; it puts the practical issue of *deciding what we should do* at the forefront. The basic issue now is not "Does God exist?" as such, but "*Should we accept* that he exists—is it appropriate to *endorse* this proposition?" The skeptic is right in maintaining that theorizing reason leaves the issue undecided. Nevertheless, in practical matters indecision yields an inactivity tantamount to negation: to suspend judgment is, in its practical effect, to resolve the issue in the negative. And, so Pascal insists, we cannot afford the comfort of suspended judgment: "A bet must be laid. There is no option: You have joined the game."

2. The Wager Argument

Let us examine Pascal's Wager argument. For convenience in analyzing its line of thought his continuous discussion can be divided into six component sectors:

> 1. Who then can blame Christians for not being able to give a logical reason for their belief, professing as they do a religion which they cannot explain by reason? They declare, when expounding it to the world, that it is a foolishness, *stultitia.* And

then you complain that they do not prove it! If they proved it, they would give the lie to their own words; it is in lacking proofs that they do not lack sense.

2. Let us examine this point and declare: "Either God exists, or He does not." To which view shall we incline? Reason cannot decide for us one way or the other: we are separated by an infinite gulf. At the extremity of this infinite distance a game is in progress, where either heads or tails may turn up. What will you wager? According to reason you cannot bet either way; according to reason you can defend neither proposition. . . . "Both are wrong. The right thing is not to wager at all." Yes; but a bet must be laid. There is no option: you have joined the game.

3. Which will you choose, then? Since a choice has to be made, let us see. . . . Your reason suffers no more violence in choosing one rather than the other, since you must of necessity make a choice. That is one point cleared up. But what about your happiness? Let us weigh the gain and the loss involved in wagering that God exists. Let us estimate these two possibilities; if you win, you win all; if you lose, you lose nothing. Wager then, without hesitation, that He does exist.

4. "That is all very fine. Yes, I must wager, but maybe I am wagering too much." Let us see. When there is an equal risk of winning and of losing, if you had only two lives to win, you might still wager; but if there were three lives to win, you would still have to play (since you are under the necessity of playing); and being thus obliged to play, you would be imprudent not to risk your life to win three in a game where there is an equal chance of winning and of losing. But there is an eternity of life and happiness. That being so, if there were an infinity of chances of which only one was in your favour, you would still do right to stake one to win two, and you would act unwisely in refusing to play one life against three, in a game where you had only one chance out of an infinite number, if there were an infinity of an infinitely happy life to win. But here there *is* an infinity of infinitely happy life to win, one chance of winning against a finite number of

chances of losing, and what you stake is finite. That removes all doubt as to choice; wherever the infinite is to be won, and there is not an infinity of chances of loss against the chance of winning, there are no two ways about it: you must risk all.

5. Now there is no use alleging the uncertainty of winning and the certainty of risk, or to say that the infinite distance between the certainty of what one risks and the uncertainty of what one will win equals that between the finite good, which one certainly risks, and the infinite, which is uncertain. This is not so; every player risks a certainty to win an uncertainty, and yet he risks a finite certainty to win a finite uncertainty, without offending reason. . . . For the uncertainty of winning is proportionate to the certainty of what is risked, according to the proportion of the chances of gain and loss. Hence, if there are as many chances on one side as on the other, the right course is to play even; and then the certainty of the risk is equal to the uncertainty of the gain, so far are they from being infinitely distant. Thus our proposition is of infinite force when there is the infinite at stake in a game where there are equal chances of winning and losing, [10] but the infinite to be won. This is conclusive, and if men are capable of truth at all, there it is.

6. . . ."But I am so made that I cannot believe. What then do you wish me to do?" . . . That is true. But understand at least that your inability to believe is the result of your passions; for although reason (now) inclines you to believe, you cannot do so. Try therefore to convince yourself, not by piling up proofs of God, but by subduing your passions. . . . You desire to attain faith, but you do not know the way. You would like to cure yourself of unbelief, and you ask for remedies. Learn from those who were once bound and gagged like you, and who now stake all that they possess. They are men who know the road that you desire to follow, and who have been cured of a sickness of which you desire to be cured. Follow the way by which they set out, acting as if they already believed, taking holy water, having masses said, etc. Even this will naturally cause you to believe and blunt your cleverness. "But that is what I fear." Why? What have you to lose?

Let us trace the flow of the argument point by point. It runs roughly as follows:

1. There is a strong streak of skepticism in Pascal—but not of irrationalism. Pascal is not concerned to downgrade reason per se—nor even to deny it a role in theology. Nor did he espouse the heresy of Fideism and maintain that proofs for the existence of God have no place whatsoever in the theological scheme of things.[11] But one can only reason effectively from conceded premises, and in this apologetic context we can expect no substantial concessions. Theological reasoning is thus inadequate to the needs of apologetics—it cannot reach those who move on a purely mundane level. From the apologetic point of view those *preuves de Dieu métaphysiques,* Pascal tells us in sect. 381/543 of the *Pensées,* are simply useless: they are too complicated and too remote from the way people ordinarily reason. Pascal does not disdain or dislike theoretical reason.[12] He is *not* a misologist. (How could so fine a mathematician and scientist be?!) He simply thinks that there are important tasks that theoretical reason cannot accomplish satisfactorily—that of demonstrating the fundamentals of the Christian religion to skeptical nonbelievers among them. He does not want us to abandon theoretical reason but simply to recognize that it has limits.[13] Reason itself requires this recognition of us: "The highest achievement of reason is to recognize that there is an infinity of things beyond its grasp" (*Pensées,* 373/267).

2. The question of inaugurating belief in God should thus be approached from a different angle—not that of constraining conviction but of motivating a *decision.* While theoretical, probative reason fails us in this apologetic context, practical reason can achieve a great deal. (Skepticism thus accomplishes something positive and useful in clearing the way for the crucial shift from theoretical to practical reason.) The issue is to be seen as one of choice under uncertainty, of a gamble with

regard to belief or nonbelief. We return to the pragmatic justification of belief mooted by the praxis-oriented thinkers of the Middle Academy. Even as the exigencies of action force physicians and engineers to judgments going beyond the limits of a firm theoretical footing, so with other pressing issues in life we must resolve our questions in ways that outrun the resources of abstract cognition. Here we are, emplaced in this world *in medias res*—like it or not. The decision whether or not to accept that God exists, and that life extends beyond the grave, confronts us unavoidably. Our disadvantaged place in the world's dispensation, and the importance and urgency the issue has for us, leaves us no alternative here as regards "playing the game." We have to opt one way or the other; the issue is simply too pressing to be relegated to the limbo of suspended judgments—it represents an option which (in William James's terms) is *living* and *momentous.* Moreover, it is *forced* as well; we cannot assume indifference—to be indifferent is effectively to come down on one side: suspension of belief is tantamount to disbelief.[14]

3. In the choice between accepting and rejecting God reason as such is unavailing: "Reason cannot make you choose either; reason cannot prove either wrong."[15] Since the question does not admit of effective resolution in the province of evidential reason, we are entitled to resolve it in the province of *interest.* And here Pascal has it that a clear advantage lies with belief. This line of deliberation is helpfully approached by considering a dominance argument. The options stand roughly as follows:

	Returns to the chooser	
Options	if God exists	if God doesn't exist
Bet on God (cost B)	$+\infty$	0
Bet against God (cost 0)	little or nothing (perhaps even something negative)	0

Betting on God clearly affords the better option here, for comparison of the two columns shows that it "dominates" over its rival in that its returns are in some cases better and in none worse than those of the alternative. If the choice stood on this basis, its resolution would be very straightforward: if you win, you win all; if you lose, you lose nothing—*"Si vous gagnez, vous gagnez tout; si vous perdez, vous ne perdez rien."*[16]

But this argument, as it stands, has a serious flaw. It fails to take account of the *cost (B)* of "betting on God," the price we pay for ordering our lives on religious principles—saying all those prayers, performing all those good works, etc. And here, in accepting that God exists and acting as he commands, the *libertin* realizes that he pays a price in giving up his self-indulgent ways. "I may perhaps wager too much." But how much is too much?

Consider an arbitrary gamble the following lines;

	Returns to the chooser	
Options	if outcome is favorable (probability p)	if outcome is unfavorable (probability $1-p$)
Bet	X	$-Y$
Do not bet	0	0

The expected value of these two alternatives stands as follows:

$$\text{Bet: } p(X) + (1-p)(-Y) = p(X+Y) - Y$$

Do not bet: 0

Now if betting costs us $\$B$, then this simply decreases the expected value of that (top) alternative by just exactly the amount B. But if X is large enough, this will not affect matters significantly. And if the value of a favorable result is relatively infinite ($X = +\infty$), as is presumably so in the theological case, then the expected value of the "Bet" alternative is also $+\infty$ as long as p is nonzero. No finite price whatsoever is now too high. "Wager, then, without hesitation."

This worry about wagering too much is crucial to the

development of Pascal's line of argumentation. For it means that straightforward dominance considerations will not suffice and recourse to *expectations* is necessary. The Wager argument thus unfolds in two stages, the second of which removes a limitation or oversimplification of its predecessor. The first step is a dominance argument. The second, by taking account of costs, shifts the issue from one of straightforward dominance to one of preponderant expectations.

At this stage Pascal's argument is effectively complete. Its job is done. The succeeding part of the discussion simply tries to show that this line of reasoning does indeed conform to the standard principles of probabilistic decision under conditions of uncertainty: the wager is simply an instance of the general strategy of probabilistic decision.

4. The next phase of deliberation proceeds in terms of the model of a lottery. However, it envisages a sequence of cases, and not just one. In each case you "stake your life" as the price of entry (the price of a ticket) and stand to win additional lives. The cases run as follows:

Case 1.

Win: gain one extra life—have two lives
Lose: lose your life—have zero lives

If there are two tickets (equal-risk case), the expected value stands as follows:

$$EV = \tfrac{1}{2}(2) + \tfrac{1}{2}(0) = 1$$

Since the expected return just equals the entry fee, "you might still play or you might not."

Case 2.

Win: gain two extra lives—have three lives
Lose: lose your life—have zero lives

Again, if there are two tickets (equal-risk case), the expected value stands as follows:

$$EV = \tfrac{1}{2}(3) + \tfrac{1}{2}(0) = 1\tfrac{1}{2}$$

Since the expectation *exceeds* the entry fee, "you would be imprudent" not to accept this gamble.

But consider now the case of an infinitely great return:

Case 3.

Win: gain eternal life (in heaven)—have infinitely many (∞) lives
Lose: lose your life—have zero lives

As long as there is a finite number (n) of tickets ("a finite number of chances of loss"), the expected value stands as follows:

$$\text{EV} = 1/n(+\infty) + \frac{n-1}{n}\ (0) = +\infty$$

Provided there is some finite chance of winning—however small—the expected return infinitely exceeds the entry fee, and the gamble should be run.

What is thus contemplated is a lottery of the following sort, with the returns indicated in "life units":[17]

	God exists (probability: $\frac{1}{n+1}$)	*God does not exist* (probability: $\frac{n}{n+1}$)
Bet on God	∞	0
Bet against God	1	1

Since the top alternative has an infinite expectation (regardless of the magnitude of n), while its rival has the uniform expectation of a single unit, betting on God is clearly the best plan. "There is no need to hesitate; you must risk all." The lesson is simple. The reasoning at issue in the Wager argument is merely an instance of the standard process of probabilistic decision on the basis of expected-value calculations. Q. E. D.

Pascal's reference to the prospect of gaining many lives is in one way misleading. The difference in value relates not merely to temporal extent (finite vs. infinite lifespan), but to the "quality of life" reflected in the great gulf which separates travail in this "vale of tears" from infinite bliss. (The value of infinitely extended mundane life might well not be infinite—repetition is boring.)

Critics of Pascal are often misled by that supposition of "equal chances of winning and losing" in para. 5. They rightly protest against any (clearly fanciful) use of the principle of indifference to arrive at one-half as representing the chance of God's existence.[18] But this objection is entirely misdirected against Pascal. His reliance on the 50:50 case is only illustrative and methodological. It plays no substantive role whatsoever in the actual argument. Nowhere does Pascal say that the probability of God's existence is one-half, and nothing in his argumentation requires it. All that matters for his reasoning is that this probability be nonzero. As long as there is a finite chance of God's existence—no matter how small—the expectation of the "bet-and-believe" alternative outweighs that of its rival.

The salient fact, then, is that Pascal's discussion at this fourth stage is simply concerned to make the point that

Figure 1

The Structure of Choice in Pascal's Wager Argument

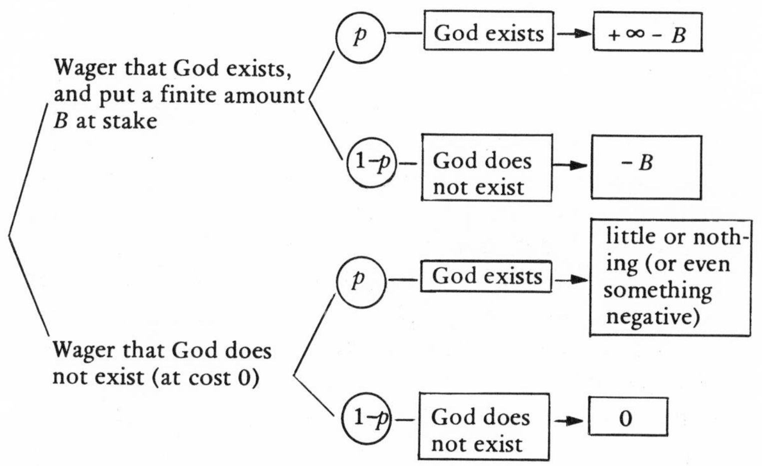

the reasoning of the Wager can easily and smoothly be accommodated by the standard mechanisms of probabilistic decision theory.[19] In its full generality the choice situation contemplated in Pascal's Wager argument takes the form set out in Figure 1. His reasoning pivots on the fact that the expected value of the top alternative—the sum of the several prospective gains/losses proportioned by the probability of their realization—is going to be $+\infty$ in any event. As long as the probability p of God's existence is nonzero, and the size of the stake B finite, the top alternative is bound to prevail in a comparison of expectations: regardless of B's specific size it produces the maximum net expected gain.

This recourse to expectations brings the central role of uncertainty to the fore. Pascal's reasoning is only in a position to persuade someone who believes that God *may* exist.[20] If the issue could be settled one way or another by theoretical argumentation (so that we know that $p = 0$ or $p = 1$), then this entire process of probabilistic argumentation would become unnecessary and pointless. The viability of this whole recourse to decision-theoretic argumentation rests on a certain incapacity, a certain ignorance. And just this ignorance, so Pascal insists, is an inherent aspect of the human condition.

5. But what can be said of the objection that in taking the gamble at issue in the Wager argument we risk a certain loss (the comforts of a self-centered and worldly life) against an uncertain gain (divine rewards). The answer is that this is an inevitable and pervasive feature of all gambling situations (lotteries, insurance, etc.). Here we *standardly* use mathematical expectations as our guide. And accordingly, Pascal reasons, as long as we are guided by the established rational gambler's standard of expected returns, we are bound to bet on God's existence. For a gamble is advantageous on the basis of this expected-value standard whenever:

$$\frac{\text{chance of winning}}{\text{chance of losing}} > \frac{\text{cost of stake}}{\text{size of prize}} = \frac{\text{potential loss}}{\text{potential gain}}$$

And if the potential gain is infinite, this standard favors the gamble as long as the chance of winning is nonzero.

To judge matters on this basis is—so Pascal insists—entirely fitting and proper. It simply applies to the particular case at hand the general principles of probabilistic decision theory that govern the rational resolution of practical choices in conditions of uncertainty.

6. The argument, of course, only shows what the rational man *should* do—that he would be well-advised (self-interestedly speaking) to become a believer. But what if one cannot manage it? What if rationality alone does not suffice to move someone? Then he can simply take various practical steps to induce himself to go whither reason points. The inducing of belief itself is a technical matter in the psychology of self-persuasion and not necessarily a matter of *reasoning* at all. The Wager argument as such—that is, as an argument—does not touch it. The job of the Wager argument is simply to establish that belief is rationally warranted. We now step outside the province of the argument as such into the region of effective praxis—of practical steps needed to give effect to its deliberations. At this point we must supplement reasoned reflection with the psychology of self-management, for a person is not only a thinking being but an animal as well, and thus (as Descartes teaches) has a mechanical side.[21] Habit can lead the mind where it is unwilling to go of itself: a reluctant person can be *made* to go where reason dictates, can be trained and rendered docile ("*vous abêtira*").

Pascal realized perfectly well that belief as such is something that lies beyond volition and cannot be constrained. But he stresses that once we recognize that belief is rationally warranted, we can and should set out to induce it. "I am so made that I cannot believe (i.e., cannot *constrain* belief). What then would you have me do?" The hypothetical respondent here concedes the weight of the Wager argument and grants its conclusion that belief is the reasonable thing. He says, "I admit that's what I *ought* to do, but I really don't think I can get myself to do it." Pascal's reply here is the recommendation to submit, that you can cure unbelief as others have done, by acting as if you believe until you finally come to do so: "Follow the way by which they begin . . . taking holy water, having masses said"—and, above all, by joining a community of believers.[22] Custom is man's very nature and can lead him to belief where all else fails.

This point is important. It is often objected against Pascal that it makes no sense to wager with belief. For, as philosophers from Hume onwards insist,[23] belief is not something at our disposal: whether or not we actually believe something does not lie within our control. Is this not fatal to Pascal's conclusion?

In response to this objection it is sometimes replied that while we cannot control what we believe, we can control what we *try* to believe or to come to believe (or else what we accept as a basis for action.)[24] But this inherently plausible line is beside the point. For while the objection that belief as such does not lie in our control is perfectly true, it is entirely irrelevant to the thrust of Pascal's argument. The argument does not issue in the injunction "Believe *P*!" but in the recommendatory finding "It would be well-advised for you to believe *P*." Its concern is not directed at belief per se at all. The pivotal issue is: What is *rational* for someone to believe? The argument simply maintains that a certain belief is reasonable (appropriate, rationally warranted). The fact that someone might (through foolishness or weakness of will) fail to believe something which he recognizes as rationally deserving of credence is entirely irrelevant and immaterial to the argument as such.

In sum, it is not the task of the Wager argument to constrain actual belief (no mere argument could achieve that!). Nor is it to motivate a course of action "as if" one believed. If practice rather than faith constituted the sum total of our religiosity, belief would be beside the point and by hypocrisy would rule the roost. (Merely to act "as if" a religion were true is, quite obviously, not really to accept that religion at all.) Rather, the Wager argument's task is to show that belief is rationally warranted—in the specifically prudential (not evidential!) mode of rational warrant. For the Wager argument unabashedly portrays faith as a means to an end. The end we hope to attain is represented by the Christian idea of salvation in an afterlife. The means necessary for attaining this end, at least according to that conception of the God which is a "live option" for us, involves a life of Christian piety and religious practice. Since faith is an integral component in such a life, its pragmatic justification follows.

*****

One recent critic writes:

> A . . . fault of Pascal's argument is this. Pascal assumes that all men would evaluate in the same way as he the various outcomes. But in fact, rightly or wrongly, men will put very different values from each other on the different outcomes. Life in the Christian heaven appeals to some more than others, and the life of worldly bliss enjoyed by the non-believer also appeals to some more than others.[25]

Two points must be made in reply. (1) Pascal makes no assumption whatsoever about how all men would evaluate outcomes. His argument is simply addressed to those who do actually have a certain evaluative stance. The person who—like Milton's Satan—does not find the prospect of eternal life in a Christian heaven appealing is obviously not going to be motivated by Pascal's Wager. But there is nothing in this that need trouble Pascal. (2) Agreement on the exact *size* of values is wholly unnecessary to the argument. All that matters is the rough and ready consideration that the magnitude of the value of the heavenly alternative is "incomparably greater" than that of the mundane —something effectively infinite by comparison. Moreover, Pascal insists that one must also reckon with the consideration that once faith is secured, then *ex post facto* the value of the "sacrifice" we make for the religious life (at cost *B*) comes to be reduced or annihilated: those worldly pleasures then come to be seen as hollow and devoid of real value. "[Y] ou will come to recognize your stake to have been laid for something certain and infinite which has cost you nothing."[26]

*****

Certain of the salient features of Pascal's argumentation accordingly deserve reemphasis:

1. The Wager argument roots in doubt—in the incapacity of cognitive reason to resolve the issue. Clearly, if we could attain rational certainty one way or the other, the whole point of the argument would be lost. The deployment of probabilities and expectations would now be inappropriate, and the whole apparatus of decision-making in conditions of uncertainty would become inapplicable.

2. The argument is nondemonstrative; it does not substantiate its conclusion—the existence of God—directly. Its impetus is *noncognitivistic.* When all is said and done, we cannot, on the basis of this argument, say that *we know that God exists.* We leave the realm of certainties.

3. The argument makes the acceptance of religion a sort of *investment* that protects us against losing out on a prospect of a massive gain. It does not establish that God exists but argues that we are justified (*prudentially*

justified) in endorsing the thesis of God's existence. It exerts its practicalistic and voluntaristic appeal upon the will and does not seek to impose any rational constraint upon the intellect.

4. The argument involves a return to the position of the academic skeptics of classical antiquity. Pure theory cannot decide—reason alone dictates *isostheneia* (indeterminacy) and *epochē* (suspension of judgment). But what cognitive reason cannot decide, *interest* can. The issue must thus be resolved on grounds of practical reason—quite appropriately so because significant gains and losses are at stake. The need for rational guidance of praxis becomes paramount.

5. The argument only maintains that it is prudent (rationally advantageous) to accept (believe, have faith) that God exists. It is *prudential* and not, strictly speaking, *evidential*. Geared to interest rather than knowledge, it proceeds *ad hominem* and not *ad rem*, being directed at us (at what we would do well to accept) and not at objective reality (at the objective nature of things).

As an instrument of apologetics, the Wager argument is aimed at *motivating* belief rather than at *demonstrating* its validity—at inaugurating faith where it is lacking rather than consolidating it where it exists. It thus approaches the issue of faith in God from a "practical" point of view. It poses the issue of religious faith as a decision about the affairs of life, like the choice of a career, the purchase of a house, or the choice of an investment for one's savings. The matter becomes a question of decision regarding the prudent management of one's affairs.

*****

Of course little that is wholly new can be found under the philosophical sun. Striking anticipations of Pascal are found in various places. One is the book *De l'Immortalité de l'âme* (Paris, 1634) by his older contemporary Pierre de Silhon (c. 1600–c. 1660).[27] He held that, since both "God exists" and "God does not exist" are alike indemonstrable from the resources of cognizing reason, one should choose the religious alternative because the failure to do so invokes a personal risk—unlike its rival course. Here as elsewhere we cannot manage affairs on the basis of *démonstrations physiques* but should govern assent on the basis of *démonstrations morales.*[28] Pascal's line is much the same.

Pascal brilliantly exploits this underlying idea of risk. The core idea of Pascal's Wager is to handle the question of "betting on God"—of faith in God and in the great promises of the Christian religion—by the same means and in the same way we use to handle risk situations in gambling (e.g., a lottery) or in commercial transactions (e.g., insurance). The issue is treated as just another case of potential gain or loss under conditions of uncertainty. The argument thus brings to bear the standard machinery of practical reasoning used in decision theory, the theory of rational choice in economics, and their congeners. No doubt the question is more momentous than most others in life's affairs, but it is nevertheless to be regarded as differing from these others not in kind but in degree.

Pascal was convinced that, for persons of a certain orientation at any rate, an effective argument for religious faith can be developed along strictly practicalistic lines. His argument accordingly portrays belief in God as part and parcel of a prudential concern for the effective pursuit of appropriate ends.

*****

Pascal's argument must be regarded, in the first instance, not as a demonstration of a thesis (a *theoretical* argument) but as legitimating a practice (a *practical* argument). Only obliquely and derivatively is it thesis-validating—by justifying the acceptance of those theses that represent the preconditions of the viability of the (appropriate) practice at issue. What is at issue is the pragmatic validation of a praxis in terms of its potential benefits, which in its turn engenders an oblique, indirect validation of belief in the existence of God as a presuppositional precondition for this praxis.

This presuppositional (and, as it were, Kantian) analysis of Pascal's argumentation is helpfully clarified by contrasting it with Ian Hacking's very different consequentialist (Jamesian) construction of the Wager argument in terms of causal efficacy:

> As Pascal sees it, you either act with complete indifference to God, or you act in such a way that you will, in due course, believe in his existence and his edicts. There is no cant to Pascal. He accepts as a piece of human nature that belief is catching: if you go along with pious people . . . you will become a believer. Pascal is speaking to a man unsure whether to follow this path, or whether to be indifferent to the morality of the church. The two possible acts are not "Believe in God" and "Do not believe." One cannot decide to believe in God. One can decide to act so that one will very probably come to believe in God. Pascal calls that the wager that God is. To wager that He is not is to stop bothering about such things.[29]

On Hacking's analysis the argumentation involves two steps: (1) the pragmatic legitimation of the practice of religious observance, and (2) our counting on this practice to engender belief *as a causal product. "Allez en avant et la fois vous viendra"* is seen as the underlying idea.

But this causative construction is too crude. For what is at issue is something more subtle: a presuppositional argument to the preconditions under which alone a pragmatically validatable practice makes sense. The overall reasoning has two phases: (1) that the religious life is pragmatically warranted, and (2) that belief in God is essential to an authentic religious life. The mechanism on which the reasoning relies in its legitimation of faith is not causal conduciveness but rational presupposition.

3. Limitations of the Wager Argument

It emerges from this account of the matter that the Wager argument is subject to certain limitations (of which Pascal himself was doubtless well aware).

1. It will certainly fail to touch the convinced atheist. Someone who sets the probability of God's existence at zero will obviously not arrive at the argument's conclusion.[30]

2. Nor does the argument reach the all-out hedonist who lives for the pleasure of the moment alone. Someone who lets the future look after itself or who is prepared to dismiss future benefits entirely—who (extending the lines of Daniel Bernoulli's resolution of the St. Petersburg paradox) is prepared to set the goods and evils of the next world at nought—would also remain untouched by the argument.

3. The argument will also have no impact on the all-trusting disbeliever. It is bound to leave untouched the person who, while believing that God does not exist, thinks that he is bound to be all-forgiving if (*contra factum*) he nevertheless did—and is therefore convinced that God, did he exist, would respond to disbelief and disobedience no differently from their opposites and would thus recompense disbelief no less amply than belief. Belief cannot be recommended on the basis of interest to someone who concedes it no possibility of advantage.

4. The argument does not deal with the radical skepticism of Pyrrhonian philosophy: the theorist who denies not only knowledge (*epistēmē*) but reasonable conviction (*to pithanon*) as well. For, like any other argument, it proceeds from premises and is accordingly impotent to enjoin its conclusion on someone who does not accept them. Unless we have some views about the nature of God (for example, believe that, should he exist, he will preferentially reward those who believe in him), Pascal's reasonings will leave us untouched. It is a grave mistake to think of the argument as addressed to the all-out philosophical skeptic. Pascal's skepticism clearly has its limits in this con-

text. Precisely because he thinks that cognitive, theoretical reason cannot yield knowledge that is useful for apologetic purposes, he is prepared to fall back on practical, interest-oriented reason. Pascal's skepticism is of the sort envisioned in the Middle Academy: the fact that theoretical *knowledge* is unavailable being offset by the availability of *reasonable conviction* of just the sort by which we manage the affairs of everyday life.[31]

5. Again, the argument carries no weight with someone who disdains the whole process of expected-value calculation and rejects the idea of letting the probability of profit afford "a guide to life." The argument will only reach the prudently self-interested man who is prepared to proceed "calculatingly" in matters of self-interest in line with standard decision-theoretic principles.

6. Finally, the argument is addressed not to those who incline to rival theologies (Zoroastrian, Buddhist, etc.) that have very different ideas about the rewards of belief, but to the ordinary indifferent, noncaring Christian-in-name-only (if that). It is only in a position to reach someone who conceives of God in a particular way, and it is not addressed to those who have nonstandard ideas about the nature of God.

The Wager argument, like any other, rests on particular premises—in its case, certain suppositions about the nature of God and his possibility. And it lies in the very nature of things that no argument, however cogent, can exert rational constraint on those who do not accept its premises. This is simply a fact of life and nowise a defect or limitation of the Wager argument.

*****

Since the days of Lucretius the following sort of reasoning has been advanced by antitheists:

> Disbelief is actually beneficial. For rejection of god, and supernatural beings in general, squarely puts the respon-

sibility for our human concerns on us humans, forcing us to come to grips with our problems.

We have here an interesting inversion of Pascal's line of thought—a theological argument from interest, to be sure, but on the side of disbelief rather than belief. In principle this sort of table-turning is fair enough. But this particular argument turns out to be specious—against Christianity at any rate. For the Christian God neither meddles in human affairs in the manner of the Greek gods on Mount Olympus nor manages them altogether in the manner of the fate decreed by an oriental-style God-potentate. He neither creates our problems nor relieves us of the task of grappling with them. Of course, where the God at issue is conceived of in a way substantially different from that of standard Christianity, the Wager argument can make no impact.

4. The Wager Argument as an Instrument of Apologetics

But what of the person who sets all those supposedly splendid benefits of salvation at zero? What if my value structure accounts the prospect of error in religious matters as catastrophic and sets the attainment of heavenly bliss at naught? Or what if the very possibility of false belief is repulsive to me, and I commit myself to evidential rigor *à outrance* and *ruat coelum.* Then well and good—so be it. The Wager argument will leave me unmoved. If one is that sort of person (but then how many of us are?), this whole line of reasoning will pass us by. Still it nowise, of course, injures the argument as such. As we have seen, the argument can only be expected to touch those who endorse its basic commitments—who accept its premises, as it were.

Here it is necessary to bear the apologetic purposes of the Wager argument in mind. Pascal's discussion is directed at *l'homme moyen sensuel,* the ordinary, self-centered "man of the world" preoccupied with his own well-being and his own prudential interests. Pascal does not address the already converted, but the glib worldly cynic—the free-thinking *libertin* of his day, the sort of persons who populated the social circle in which Pascal himself moved prior to his conversion.[32] The format of the discussion is that of a dialogue with just such a person. And it is part of the tacit ground rules of the discussion that there is to be no appeal to faith, to religious experiences, to authority—to any evidence that goes beyond man's "natural light." Pascal's concern is thus with the rational justification of an action through an appeal to self-interest.

The aim of Pascal's Wager argument is one of apologetics and not of theological theorizing. And, even here, it is a special-purpose instrument with a limited and special mission—to stiffen the backbone of the slack and worldly Christian. The convinced atheist, the radical philosophical skeptic, the all-out hedonist, the all-trusting disbeliever, and those otherwise predisposed toward alien theological systems will not (and are not intended to) be reached by this mode of argumentation. These other battles of apologetics must be fought on other fronts with other weapons.

In view of its status as an appeal to self-interest, many commentators have felt that Pascal's Wager argument is altogether beneath the dignity of serious religiosity and unworthy of a religious thinker deserving of this name. But this line of objection loses sight of the job that Pascal actually intends the argument to do. His deliberations are intended to motivate *l'homme moyen sensuel* into making a start at religious faith, and his pivotal question is this: What line of thought could prove effective in bringing the nominally Christian but actually slack, indifferent, and worldly outsider into the fold of believers? If we fail to reckon with the apologetic purpose of the argument as delineated in these terms, we will not be in a position to evaluate it appropriately.

The standard supporting pillars of the edifice of Christian belief are much as Table 1 indicates. Most of these have serious drawbacks from the standpoint of apologetics.

Table 1

Routes to the Legitimation of Faith

REASON

- Cognitive/evidential reasoning; rational demonstration (the reasonings of the Church Fathers, the scholastic doctors, Descartes)
- Practical reasoning

CUSTOM

- Group tradition: the collective testimony of the church: the "cloud of witnesses" in the history of ongoing commitment (the attestation of the living church and the witness of the faithful)
- Cultural habituation in education and acculturation

EXPERIENCE

- Personal experience (inspiration): the "call" of the prophets, the insight of the mystics, or the believer's contact with God in prayer
- Revelation (as transmitted vicariously through the prophets or scriptures)

Revelation generally speaks only to the already converted. Most ordinary men do not have the right sort of experience: personal religious experience exerts its impetus only on the select. The church's testimony leaves the "outsider" cold. Cultural habituation often points a contrary way. And while it might seem that rational demonstration is the best prospect given the universal cogency of its appeal, it too has its problems. For it is precisely when the argumentation is at its most tight and rigorous that it cannot lead beyond the reach of conceded premises—whose availability cannot be supposed in the present context. As Pascal sees it, practical reasoning prevails in apologetics *faute de mieux,* for want of a better alternative.

Following Montaigne and the Renaissance tradition of Christian skepticism, Pascal insists that the sorts of proofs and demonstrations by which scholastic thinkers and their congeners sought to validate actual *knowledge (epistēmē)* in the best Platonic and Stoic manner are simply not available for apologetic purposes. Indeed, such demonstrative arguments *are not even desirable,* because the features of God accessible to demonstrative reason alone could not suffice to enable him to answer to the needs of the human condition. In the setting of apologetics we would not even want a demonstrable God if we could have one, because the "God of the philosophers" cannot speak to the condition of the plain man. This line of thought impels Pascal into giving his apologetics a pragmatic cast.

Is pragmatically based acceptance a different sort of acceptance from that based on evidential considerations and purely epistemic criteria? Of course it is! But is the acceptance of something on a different basis not tantamount to acceptance of something different! By no means! If I accept that $\sqrt{2} \cong 1.41$, I accept exactly the same thing (the same fact) regardless of whether I read it in a textbook, am told it by someone, or figure it out for myself. The difference at issue here is purely epistemic. It relates not in any way to the substantive *content* of the belief, but only to the nature of the considerations that provide warrant for its acceptance. The *substance* of acceptance is wholly unaffected by its *grounds*: differences in point of grounding do not make for differences in what is accepted. An accepted claim is what it is regardless of its basis. If I accept that "Ten people are in the room," it is substantively indifferent whether I count them myself, or monitor their presence by scanners, or learn of their presence from the reports of others. Its epistemic basis does not affect the *content* of the claim. Whatever the *grounds* on which I accept *P* as true, it is still *P* that I accept. In accepting a thesis we add its substantive content to the stock of our information. From this point of view its *grounding* is immaterial. (Grounding is a matter not of *what* but of *why*.)

How one comes by a conviction does not affect its object; that which we find is unaffected by how we found it. (To think otherwise is to commit what has come to be called "the genetic fallacy.") Still it is bound to affect our *attitude* toward what we find. How we argue for God is bound to condition how we think of him. It is not that with different arguments we establish a different God, but rather that our attitude toward the God we establish is bound to be affected. (It is the same sum of money whether we get it by hard work or by winning a lottery, but our stance toward it is bound to differ.) When we argue for God in a certain way, the God we argue for is bound to be seen in the light of the kind of argumentation we offer; our view of God will inevitably reflect the route through which we reach him—though the issue is clearly not one of a different God but merely of a different way of regarding him. The matter of attitude is crucial in the present religious context: with religious beliefs the issues of content and attitude are bound to intermingle.

For Pascal a leading positive attraction of the Wager argument is thus its negative aspect: its turning away from outright demonstration and its abandonment of any claims to purely rational compulsion. In his view an apologetically effective argument cannot and must not even seek to *demonstrate.* Rather, it should *motivate* in the practical order of things. And this shift from cognition to praxis is the pivot of the Wager argument.

*****

The wider implications of Pascal's shift can be brought out by contrasting two questions:

(1) Does God exist?

(2) Is it *X* (prudent or high-minded or foolish, etc.) *to believe that* God exists.

Clearly (2) brings very different issues upon the scene: not only God alone but also the basis of belief and the nature of *X* (prudence or foolishness or whatever).

Pascal's discussion is predicated on the conviction that (1) as such is effectively intractable in the context of apologetics: And so he shifts the discussion to (2), subject to the particular construction that the *X* at issue is a matter of prudence. His argumentation is predicated on the necessity of transposing the issue of religious apologetics from the sphere of cognitive (inquiring) reasoning to that of prudential or practical reasoning.

To be sure, from every purely this-worldly point of view —material, social, and psychological—our interest is strongly engaged on the side of disbelief. As *this* world runs—to all appearances—every mundane advantage lies with disbelief. That is why Pascal calls, Canning-like, upon the next world to redress the wrongs of this one.

The argumentation of Pascal's Wager seeks to validate religious belief not as a *system of knowledge* (a theology), but rather as a *program of life*—though, to be sure, one that has profound consequences for belief. It hews to the line that such a program can reasonably be adopted (at any rate initially) on pragmatic/prudential grounds—on grounds of advantage (be it, with Pascal, with a view to advantage in the next world, or with William James, with a view to advantage in this one).

Pascal thus sees the best hope of effective apologetics to lie in the sphere of practical reasoning. To be sure, other instruments—demonstration included—will have their use in other departments of theology. In Pascal's view, none of the traditional sources of probative authority in religion can be set aside entirely—on its own ground each has a proper job to do; once we have entered into the province of faith, all the various routes to its legitimation have some part to play.[33] But the most fundamental job (in the sense of "first things first") is that of practical reason. It is certainly not of the "highest" authority. But given the disposition of the audience and the imperfect nature of the human condition, it is the place where Christian apologetics can best make its start.

5. The Import of the Wager Argument: The Probabilistic Turn

Theological argumentation from self-interest with a view to the prospect of gain or loss was of course not invented by Pascal. Homilists had been going on in this vein for centuries. After all, if even *Paris vaut bien la messe,* how can one balk at the prospect of attaining heaven?

Again, the idea of prudent choice under uncertainty was not really new in this context. A century before Pascal, St. Thomas More told the anecdote of the courtier and the poor cleric:

> And it fareth betwene these two kynde of folke as it fared betwene a lewde galante and a pore frere. Whom when the galante saw going barefote in a great frost and snowe, he asked him why he did take such payn. And he aunswered that it was very little payn, if a man would remember hell. Ye frere, quoth the galante, but what and there be none hell? Then art thou a great foole. Ye maister, quoth the frere, but what and there be hell? Then is youre maistershyppe a much more foole?[34]

Already the Christian theologian Arnobius, who flourished in the reign of Diocletian (284–305), wrote in his apologetic tract *Adversus gentes* as follows:

> [T]here can be no proof of things still in the future. Since then, the nature of the future is such that it cannot be grasped and comprehended by any anticipation, is it not more rational, of two things uncertain and hanging in doubtful suspense, rather to believe that which carries with it some hopes (*quod aliquas spes ferat*) than that which brings none at all? For in the one case there is no danger if that which is said to be at hand should prove vain and groundless; in the other there is the greatest loss, even the loss of salvation, if, when the time has come, it eventuates that our expectation was erroneous.[35]

Prudentialism in the face of risk and uncertainty, then, is nothing new in religious discourse.

But there is an important element in Pascal's argumentation that was wholly new and original: the concept of a *measured* gamble, a probabilistically *calculated* risk. Such a deployment of probabilistic reasoning with its use of the decision-theoretic tactic of guiding action on "the balance of probabilities" was something quite novel. This innovative recourse to gambling, probability, and the doctrine of chances—to that decision-theoretic employment of the calculus of probabilities which was Pascal's own invention[36]—illustrates yet again the common phenomenon of bringing new intellectual tools to bear on old problems that are encountered in all departments of intellectual endeavor.

In this regard John Locke's reasoning goes badly awry. Locke argues in Pascal-reminiscent style that a life of *virtue* (rather than religiosity) is preferable under a bare possibility of an afterlife:

> He that will allow exquisite and endless happiness to be but the possible consequence of a good life here and the contrary state the possible reward of a bad one . . . must conclude [that a virtuous life is to be adopted]. I have foreborne to mention anything of the certainty or probability of a future state, designing here to show the wrong judgment that anyone must allow he makes . . . who prefers the short pleasures of a vicious life upon any consideration whilst he knows, and cannot but be certain, that a future life is at least possible.[37]

As Locke sees it, the possibility of an infinite reward outweighs the possibility of a finite one, wholly apart from any probabilistic considerations. The view seems to be that if only the stake is big enough, one should go ahead and "take the chance and go for broke"—probabilities need not enter in. But whatever the merits (or demerits) of this view, it is not the position that is at issue in Pascal's deliberations. For him the probabilistic aspect is crucial.

Many treatments of the Wager argument evince discomfort about *any* recourse to mathematics—Pascal's included. As one recent commentator puts it:

> By his introduction of mathematics into the argument Pascal added the subtilty and curiosity of the argumentation, but it may be questioned whether he has thereby added to its form and value. . . . [T]o many his mathematics can be a factor that detracts from the persuasive and hortatory character of the whole. The mathematicizing is too elaborate and too subtle to add strength to the appeal that the argument is designed to make.[38]

One wonders where this author got his information about "the appeal that the argument is designed to make." Surely not from Pascal's discussion itself, which makes it clear as crystal that the argument is not designed to be popular, to appeal to "the ordinary common sense of common folk." It is addressed precisely to the man who is clever and calculating, who fancies himself a shrewd person who stands above and beyond the reach of popular homiletics. The mathematical character of the argument as an exercise in decision theory is integral to the function that Pascal intends for it.

Some critics object that Pascal's argument runs into trouble at exactly this point of conjuring with probabilities. Thus Anthony Flew writes:

> Yet this apparent force [of the Wager argument] depends on a gigantic assumption, concealed and false. For it assumes that the tally of possible mutually exclusive, Hell-threatening systems is finite. . . . But this is parochial and unimaginative. . . . [And if there are infinitely many alternatives] we cannot make a reasoned bet. But with regard to the transcendent there is no limit to the range. No odds can be given. The whole idea of betting breaks down.[39]

But this objection hits wide of the mark. Pascal has no need for calculating the numerical value for the probability of God's existence from some body of raw data regarding possible alternatives. His invocation of probability here is subjectivistic, not combinatory (and is, moreover, independent of specifically quantitative valuation). For the matter turns on the way in which the Wager argument's addressee himself evaluates the prospect of God's existence.[40] Pascal's argument is simply addressed to those who see the existence of the Christian God as a *real* possibility to which they are prepared to accord a nonzero probability (however "imponderable" they may deem this quantity to be in other regards). Apart from this the numerical status of this probability—even its having a definite and stable value—is quite irrelevant.

And this fact has important ramifications. Hume held that we cannot accept the testimony of an interested witness, and Laplace decked this view out with mathematical argumentation. If the witness has a great personal stake on the side of the question his testimony supports, the temptation for him to lie is great—indeed asymptotically infinite. And so the biblical stories transmitted by the earliest Christians are doubtful in the extreme—they lack even a finite probability. Laplace saw this point as fatal to Pascal's position[41] —and so indeed it might be if it established that the existence of the Christian God is of probability zero.[42] But Laplace's view is of questionable soundness. From the two premises

– X claims that he has good evidence for maintaining p (e.g., that he saw this with his own eyes)

and

– X lies; he actually has no good evidence but spoke from interest alone

nothing whatsoever follows regarding the probability of p itself. The probability of the substance of a claim is wholly unaffected by the fact that those who make the claim have no adequate warrant for it and are actually ignorant in the matter at hand. I ask Smith whether heads will come up on the next toss of coin. He replies brazenly, "I know that it won't—I have infallible foresight in these matters." Let it be granted that he is lying through his teeth. Does that make the probability of heads zero?[43] The Laplacean argument turns on the equivocation of "lie" = *speak falsely as to the* FACT *of one's claims,* on the one hand, and "lie" = *speak falsely as to the* JUSTIFICATION *of one's claims,* on the other. The circumstance that an interested witness may well "lie" in this second sense may plausibly disincline us from accepting his testimony. But it does nothing whatever to establish the falsity—or improbability—of his claims. (We can get no further then the Scots' verdict, "not proven.")

In arguing against Pascal's wager, Laplace in effect casts the church in the role of a set of interested Witnesses who say: "Pay the price P and I can promise you on God's behalf that he will give you a great reward R."[44] Laplace now argues as follows. If we do as the Witnesses say, we confront the pay-off situation:

The Witnesses speak truly (probability p)	*The Witnesses speak falsely* (probability $1-p$)
$R - P$	$-P$

The expected value of this action will now be

$$\mathrm{EV} = p(R - P) + (1 - p)(-P) = pR - P$$

Pascal tries to assure that this is infinite by setting R at ∞. But this, Laplace now insists, is a mistake. For p and R should be presumed to be *interdependent*: the bigger the reward R the Witnesses promise us, the less, so we are to suppose, is the likelihood that they speak truly. Suppose that, in fact,

$$pR = \text{constant} = \tfrac{1}{2}P$$

Then the expectation at issue will in fact be uniformly negative; it will be $-\tfrac{1}{2}P$.

Laplace's counterargument is fine as far as it goes. But it does not really tell against Pascal's position. For it pivots crucially on the "fish-story principle": the bigger the claim, the less likely its truth. Now this may be very well in its place, but its place is not in theology. It just won't do to say that gods who promise less are *ipso facto* more likely. The apologetic context at issue will have to define the parameters of the operative god-conception, and it is this that must set the stage of our deliberations. Issues regarding the creditability of witnesses are beside the point.

Pascal certainly does not base his view that the probability of God's existence is nonzero on the testimony of the early Christians. On the contrary, he insists that such testimony is effectively unavailable for apologetic purposes. His own starting point is skepticism—we must suppose that nothing apologetically useful can be established one way or the other through evidence and factual deliberation. We must simply implement our subjective inclination to acknowledge that the possibility exists. We must, in the final analysis, come to terms with *our own ideas* about God.

This aleatory aspect of Pascal's innovation was no less shocking and offensive to contemporary ideology and received opinion than its prudential orientation. Cries of outrage had greeted Thomas Gataker's 1616 essay "On the Nature and Use of Lots" which defended the lawfulness of lots when not used for divination, and which led to violent attacks on its author as an advocate for unsavory games of hazard.[45] Even a century after the Wager argument was propounded, Voltaire (of all people!) objected to Pascal's *infini-rien* discussion: "This article seems a little indecent and puerile; the idea of a game, and of loss and gain, does not benefit the gravity of the subject."[46] Gambling was deemed a distinctly disreputable activity in those times. Pascal's friend, the clever but somewhat shady Chevalier de Méré, was deplored by the pious as a typical specimen of the wordly *libertin*: "brilliant talker, fearless freethinker, and inveterate gambler."[47] Yet it is exactly this sort of person that Pascal set out to address in the Wager argument.

The choice of his intended audience represented a departure altogether characteristic of Pascal's view of the human condition. As he saw it, *man is not respectable*—his motivation is base, his thought calculating. Effective apologetics must begin by moving down to man's own natural level; it must reach him in the base region that is his natural habitat. To do effectively the job that needs to be done, it must fight fire with fire. (To be sure, this is not the end of the matter; never for an instant did Pascal deem this appeal to interest more than the start of a much longer and ultimately very different story.) Pascal's Wager is an appeal neither to man's scientific prowess (to competence at factual inquiry) nor to his "better self" (to human idealism), but to rational self-interest. As he saw it, the religious journey will no doubt eventually lead to a certainty of higher principle but can (and for many must) begin in the moral certitude of man's practical affairs.

*****

Pascal can thus lay claim to a watershed innovation. To be sure, the theory of practical reason is as old as Aristotle. And the invocation of considerations of *praxis* to justify cognitive claims (claims perhaps not to *knowledge,* but to *warranted belief*) is as old as the Neo-Platonic semi-skepticism of the Middle Academy.[48] But Pascal's inventiveness came to the fore in his resort to considerations of calculated choice under conditions of uncertainty, made feasible by the nascent calculus of probability in whose development he himself played an important part. And this practicalistic turn is crucial for his purposes. For his aim is to show that religious belief cannot only be *reconciled* with the sorts of considerations on whose basis we conduct life's affairs but can even be *supported* by them. This circumstance, as we shall see, helps Pascal to blunt various sorts of objections to his apologetic argumentation.

6. Subsequent Developments

The use of practical reasoning in theology represents a path that was to be followed by such later thinkers as

Immanuel Kant, William James, and Hans Küng in ways critically important for their characteristic positions.

Kant. The primacy of practical over theoretical reason is evident at various key points in Kant's philosophy. As Kant saw it, the building blocks of man's theoretical cognition are rooted in postulates that reflect the operational requirements of human thought rather than characterizing a mind-independent reality. This is true in particular (though by no means only) in the domain of theology. Here we must reject *knowledge* to make way for *faith.* We have no feasible way of *demonstrating* the existence of God. The ground of our belief in God is not *cognitive* (theoretical, "speculative") at all, but wholly *practical,* geared not to proofs but to an analysis of the requisites of rationally appropriate *praxis* in its various dimensions (inquiry, morality, evaluation).

Thus Kant's critical stress on the limitations of pure (theoretical/speculative) reason serves exactly the same function as Pascal's skepticism—viz., to clear the way for a resource other than inquiring reason as such. In both cases alike this resource is broadly *practical* (though in Kant's case it is preeminently moral, while in Pascal's case it is, given his apologetic concerns, preeminently prudential).

The relation of Kant's thought to Pascal's can be viewed in the following terms. With Pascal we have the line of reasoning:

- Considerations of practical advantage for us humans can indicate the appropriateness of belief in God.
- *Therefore*: belief in God is legitimated in the specifically prudential mode of rational deliberation.

With Kant this line of thought evolves into a more sophisticated form:

- Human endeavor in all three of its modes (inquiry, action, and evaluation) presupposes belief in God as a condition of the rational possibility of goal-achievement (i.e., of science, morality, and evaluative judgment).

– *Therefore*: belief in God is legitimated in the practical domain of reason.

In Kant, the *conception* of God serves as the regulator of praxis—as guiding principle (*Leitfaden*) alike for our cognitive, our moral, and our evaluative strivings. (All three *Critiques* lead to exactly the same destination in this regard.) We do not deal with God *ontologically*—as a *being* about whom we have constitutively determinate substantive knowledge. Rather, we can and should proceed *regulatively* and, as it were, pragmatically without overt reification or hypostatization. The *concept* of God serves as an ideal which shapes our practice in inquiry, in action, and in evaluation. Faith in God is geared to praxis—the cultivation of the highest good (in any of its dimensions) presupposes belief in the existence of God as guarantor of the possibility of achieving this end. (As Kant saw it, the praxis of rational inquiry, of moral agency, and of evaluative judgment all ultimately presuppose such a belief.) Belief in God is accordingly not to be justified by a theoretical argument to validate a claim to knowledge, but rather by a transcendental argument geared to the underpinnings of a praxis.

And so with Kant, as with Pascal, the justification of *belief* in God is in the final analysis rooted in considerations of interest. The seed sown by Pascal's turning away from evidentiated knowledge and theoretical demonstration to faith and practical justification gathers a rich harvest in Kant's Critical Philosophy,[49] and one must recognize Pascal as a prime precursor in this regard:

> Thus even after reason has failed in all its ambitious attempts to pass beyond the limits of all experience, there is still enough left to satisfy us, so far as our practical standpoint is concerned. No one, indeed, will be able to boast that he *knows* that there is a God, and a future life; if he knows this, he is the very man for whom I have long (and vainly) sought. . . . No, my conviction is not *cognitive*, but *moral* certainty; and since it rests on subjective

> grounds (of the moral sentiment), I must not even say, 'It *is* morally certain that there is a God, etc.', but 'I *am* morally certain, etc.' In other words, belief in a God and in another world is so interwoven with my moral sentiment that as there is little danger of my losing the latter, there is equally little cause for fear that the former can ever be taken from me.[50]

Here the voice is Kant's but the hands are Pascal's. The fact is that, like Kant and numberless others after him, Pascal sought for a *via media* between rationalistic dogmatism and corrosive skepticism—and deemed himself to have found it in a mitigated skepticism based on practical and mundane certainty.

James. William James continued this practice-geared line of religious thought and placed it in a different context. His ideas unfolded against the background not only of Kant but also of a whole host of other practicalist influences: Peirce's pragmatism, post-Darwinian evolutionary philosophizing (e.g., Nietzsche, Spencer), and the teaching of the French relativists (Bergson, Meyerhoff) that science is an interpretation of reality attuned to the needs of practice. A common epistemological theme recurs throughout these sources: that our knowledge-claims are ultimately based on and validated through considerations of practice.

James's position in the philosophy of religion can be seen as a natural application of this general line of thought. James offers an explicit defense of "a right to believe" on pragmatic grounds.[51] Just as accepting a scientific theory involves an inductive leap that is ultimately validated by successful praxis in the laboratory, so adopting a religious position involves a "leap of faith" that is retrovalidated by successful praxis in the laboratory of life. On James's view, the legitimation of religious belief should be developed in pragmatic terms—faith is an eminently practical resource that facilitates man's way in a difficult and often unfriendly world.

James insists that our hand is not forced in important issues of life by pressures whose impetus is entirely beyond our control. We are able to make our own decisions; we are free agents. As such we face a choice—the most momentous of our whole lives. It is the choice of what sort of person we want to be—the sort of person we want to *make* of ourselves. This choice ramifies in many directions. But one of the most important of these is the option between:

1. Being a believer: having faith in the ultimate meaningfulness of our life in this world as an important part of a wider order of meaning and value.

2. Being a nonbeliever: seeing the material world as self-sufficient and denying any objective basis of value. Taking the Stoic view that man must stand alone, self-reliant against the forces of nature and history.

No demonstration from patent evidence can settle matters here. The choice is incapable of being resolved either way through knockdown, drag-out arguments. It is a profoundly practical one that we are able *and entitled* to make on the basis of practical criteria.

Where Kant saw belief in God as validated presuppositionally in terms of the practical preconditions of certain human projects (science, morality, evaluation), William James saw this belief as validated motivationally as a stimulus to the effective action that is essential to satisfactory living. Kant's analysis looks backward to presuppositions; James's, forward to consequences. But either way, considerations of praxis are pivotal.

To be sure, one big difference between Pascal and James must be stressed. It is brought out by contemplating James's thesis that:

> Our passional nature not only lawfully may, but must decide an option between propositions, whenever it is a genuine option that cannot by its nature be decided on intellectual grounds.[52]

Pascal's position differs from this in two salient ways: (1) Pascal does not invoke *passion* but *interest,* i.e., practical reason; and so he remains on the side of thought as against feeling. (2) Pascal invokes practical reason not as a tie breaker but as a gap filler; he allows practical reason to speak where inquiring reason is silent because evidence is unavailable, but not to give rulings where evidence is indeed available and balances out pro and con.[53] Pascal, like Kant, supposes a *division* of *labor* between practical and theoretical reason; he does not see practical reason as a tool to be borrowed by theoretical reason where its own resources prove insufficient.

Küng. The German theologian Hans Küng is a contemporary link in this same chain. In his massive book *Does God Exist?* he adopts a position that has many points of similarity to Pascal's.[54] He too dismisses the efficacy of demonstrations: "the probative character of the proofs of God is finished today" (pp. 535-36). He too wants to appeal beyond theoretical/evidential to practical reason and to seek "to confront man as thinking and acting with a rationally justifiable decision that goes beyond pure reason and demands the whole person" (p. 536). And he too assimilates belief in God to a fundamental trust in the cooperation of nature: "I stake myself without security or guarantee . . . either I regard reality . . . as trustworthy and realiable—or not" (p. 438). This choice, as Küng explicitly recognizes, is deeply akin to that of Pascal's Wager.

*****

The pragmatic tradition in philosophical theology thus received a powerful impetus in Pascal's turning from theoretical/demonstrative argumentation to practical reasoning. And the course of historical events that led from Kant through James to later pragmatism was to assure that this turning was not just a haphazard idiosyncracy, but a permanent gain for philosophy. In its light we may see Pascal not as an isolated eccentric, but as a key link in a long chain of praxis-oriented thinking that runs from the mitigated skeptics of the Middle Academy through Kant and William James to the amply flowing stream of contemporary thought in the pragmatic tradition.

II
The Epistemology of Pragmatic Beliefs

1. The Pragmatic Route to Belief Validation and the Complexity of Reason

William James complained that Pascal's Wager argument begins with the contention that human reason cannot tell us what to do and ends with the thesis that a certain course is clearly the reasonable one.[55] Many discussions of Pascal support this accusation of self-inconsistency. Jean Mesnard, for example, represents Pascal's argument as starting with the claim that "reason cannot determine our choice" and arriving at the conclusion that "our reason therefore commands us to bet on the existence of God."[56] But to make this sort of complaint is to fail badly to grasp what is actually going on in Pascal's deliberations. A critical distinction is overlooked. For two very distinct species of "reason" are at issue in Pascal—the *evidential* that seeks to establish facts (and is in his view entirely inadequate to the demands of apologetics) and the *practical* that seeks to legitimate actions (and can indeed justify us in "betting on God" via the practical step of *accepting* that he exists). The heart too has its *reasons.* Only by blithely ignoring this crucial distinction between evidentially fact-establishing and pragmatically action-validating reason can one press the charge of inconsistency against Pascal. Let us examine this distinction more closely.

The theory of knowledge standardly focuses upon evidential considerations and examines the ways and means by which evidence grounds our beliefs. But there is also room for another department of epistemology to deal with cognitive situations that obtain when the evidence simply fails to settle the issue one way or another. Its problem-domain is set by the question: How are we to proceed rationally and sensibly when the available evidence is "insufficient" and leaves the issue unresolved, failing to settle matters one way or the other?

Of course, one thing we can always do in this circumstance is to suspend judgment—to refrain from coming down on either side, awaiting the day when the evidential situation changes so as to resolve the issue. But, as the skeptics of classical antiquity already recognized, such suspension of belief is in many situations a luxury we cannot afford. In practical matters we may well be unable to wait for evidential reason to arrive at a resolution. Is that water safe to drink or not? Will that plank across the chasm which we must cross to escape from danger support our weight? Which of these trains will carry us to our destination? A suspension of judgment leads to inaction, and inaction may, in the circumstances, lead to catastrophe. In practical situations we may "simply have to make up our mind and take our chances." And yet we do not want to do this haphazardly. Precisely because substantial consequences are at stake, we require the guidance of rational considerations to assure us that there is due warrant for the alternative we espouse—that we have opted for what is, in the circumstances, the best available course.

As Samuel Johnson observed, so many objections might be made to everything that nothing could overcome them but the necessity of doing *something.*[57] The salient difference between "purely theoretical" and practical contexts is that in the former one can always suspend judgment without penalty, while in the latter we must make up our minds. And, seeing that in a rational animal action and belief are inseparably interlocked, we must recognize that belief (purported knowledge) has an inherently *practical* side. In fact, most of our cognitive/epistemic deliberations occur in practical settings and are thus subject to the ground-rules of practical rationality rather than those of theoretical rationality alone. And so the use of prudential considerations for purposes of informational gap-filling is perfectly appropriate from the standpoint of reason. To withhold judgment where the evidence is insufficient—and to do this always and everywhere, in season and out—is the course of folly, not of wisdom, of unreasonableness, not of "strict rationality."

*****

When we accept something on pragmatic grounds, the evidence must not stand in the way. One obviously cannot (if halfway rational) get oneself to accept *P* while all the time standing convinced of the truth of not-*P*. The aspect of *gap-filling* is crucial, and explains Pascal's insistence on a propaedeutic skepticism to clear the stage. The evidential situation must be one of *nihil obstat*: Pascal does not want to set utility against evidence. His project does *not* require him to call on us to endorse evidentially counterindicated propositions on grounds of other benefits.

The Pascal of the Wager argument is not one of those religious skeptics who write man's intellect off and pit blind faith against reason. Rather, he insists that we acknowledge the power and diversity of reason in recognizing that there is practical as well as theoretical reason.

On such an approach it is necessary to distinguish two different sorts of rational justification of beliefs: (1) the probative, as based on *evidential* reasons, and (2) the pragmatic, as based on *prudential* reasons. The contrast between the two turns on a difference in requirements of justification. A person *X* is *evidentially* justified in believing a thesis *P* when he is warrantedly persuaded that:

(1) the probability of *P* relative to the evidence at *X*'s disposal is substantial, and

(2) *P* coheres adequately with (all of the) other beliefs that *X* accepts on evidential grounds.

By contrast, *X* is *pragmatically* (and thus nonevidentially) justified in believing a thesis *P* when he is warrantedly persuaded that:

(1) The probability of *P* relative to the evidence at *X*'s disposal is nonzero.

(2) *P* is not actually incompatible with (any or all of the) other beliefs that *X* accepts on evidential grounds. There are no substantive impediments on the side of evidence, so that as far as the evidence goes, *nihil obstat.*

(3) *X* has some (otherwise reasonable and appropriate) goal whose realization is impracticable in the absence of accepting *P.*

(4) *P* coheres optimally with the other beliefs that *X* accepts on pragmatic grounds. As far as all relevant (evidential, pragmatic, social, etc.) considerations go, there is not substantial impediment to the acceptance of *P.*

Here condition (3) comes to:

(3.1) The agent has certain aims.

(3.2) These aims are (and he has good reason to believe them to be) proper and legitimate.

(3.3) The agent has cogent reason to think that adopting the belief is demanded for (or will at any rate greatly facilitate) the realization of these aims.

The justificatory rationale of a pragmatic belief lies preeminently in the circumstance that there are substantial practical grounds for its endorsement, but no strong evidential (or other) grounds against it.

To base the acceptance of propositions on practical reasons of advantage obviously has certain potential difficulties:

1. It might conflict with the contrary indications of the evidence.
2. It might lead to the endorsement of something that is objectionable on practical or moral grounds.
3. It might stand in the way of accepting something else that is even more desirable.

But where no obstacles of this sort enter in, prudentially based acceptance is certainly justifiable—to wit, *pragmatically* justifiable. And, of course, in the special case of Pascal's argument none of these obstacles to appropriateness do enter in. It is clear that none of these recognized grounds for objecting to a pragmatic argument will tell against the reasoning of Pascal's Wager.

The pragmatic approach to justification takes the stance that in certain circumstances it is (rationally) *appropriate* for an agent to have recourse to nonevidential considerations as a basis for warranting beliefs. It is a mode of justification linked to a pursuit of the good in general (and not limited to the issue of belief in God). In cases of the sort now at issue the agent has a perfectly rational basis for accepting the beliefs at issue, although, to be sure, this rationality obtains in the pragmatic order of prudential reasons rather than the evidential order of specifically probative reasons. Acceptance in such circumstances is action-facilitative rather than strictly cognitive; it reflects the needs of *praxis* rather than the requirements of *theoria.* The goal-correlative aspect of pragmatic belief endows it with an element of personal relativity. We must not say "It is certain that *P*," but "I am pragmatically certain that *P*"—as Kant perceptively remarked in an analogous situation.[58]

Belief-validation in the pragmatic mode of reasoning often takes the following specific form:

– It is sensible to do *A*.

– There is no decisive reason to think that *A* cannot be done in the prevailing circumstances.[59]

– The acceptance of *P* substantially facilitates any attempt to do *A*.

– There is no good positive reason (i.e., reason apart from the negative fact of a lack of substantiating evidence against accepting *P*).

–*Therefore*: It is (pragmatically) sensible to accept *P*.

Consider an example of this sort of argumentation: "It is sensible to try to save myself from this fire. Only if I have confidence in my ability to leap to yonder ledge can I manage this. Therefore, I am well advised to take the view that I can reach the ledge if I make a real effort." This general approach was originated by the academic skeptics of antiquity, but was developed more fully by William James in his polemic against W. K. Clifford.

Showing that a belief is evidentially well spoken for is accordingly not the only way to obtain a rational warrant for its acceptance. When the evidential circumstances are not preclusively adverse, we can reasonably accept suitably convenient theses in the presence of compellingly favorable normative/pragmatic considerations. The rational justification of beliefs can in principle proceed in the pragmatic rather than the evidential order: evidence does not have a monopoly on reason. The complaint that it is rationally irresponsible to hold a belief that is inadequately substantiated by way of evidential grounds simply overlooks that there are different orders of reason, that there are pragmatic as well as evidential modes of justification. There is nothing wrong with the unproblematic injunction "Accept only what you have good grounds for accepting." It is simply that *evidential* grounds are not the only sorts of good grounds.

This approach takes the practicalist stance that even as in other cases it is appropriate for "the prudent person" to do what is advantageous, so it is also in this matter of acceptance. It treats propositional acceptance potentially as just another possible human act—albeit one of a somewhat special sort, namely, a "cognitive act" of thesis-adoption. To be sure, the fact that a belief is pragmatically warranted does not render the claim at issue any more probable—let alone certain. It is a matter of adopting or accepting certain contentions because in the circumstances doing so demonstrably furthers the realization of one's cognitive ends—practical as well as theoretical. We are enjoined to endorse the thesis at issue not so much on evidential as on prudential grounds.

But what then of the *truth* of the belief in question? A gap clearly remains to be closed here. But of course the matter is no different in the evidential case. A well-evidentiated belief is not thereby necessarily true. (The lesson of the skeptics holds—truth and evidence are more separate and independent issues than we like to admit.[60]) There is no denying that the rational person *ex officio* subscribes to the principle of endeavoring to accept only *true* propositions.[61] But *evidence* is clearly not the only promising route to truth; there is also plausibility, analogy, coherence, etc. And there is no good reason why we cannot add *safety* to the list.

Pascal does not want us to avert our eyes from the distinction between what we know to be true and what we are well advised to think (be it for prudential or moral or other reasons). Indeed his whole argument pivots on this distinction. What matters for the Wager argument is simply that evidence does not have a corner on the market of good reasons. Of course, nobody is proposing to dismiss evidence as irrelevant in cognitive deliberations. It is a matter of resisting the reverse course of dismissing prudence as irrelevant. What is at issue is a *noncognitive* but nevertheless *nowise irrational* basis for belief. Our cognitive goals are not our only goals, so that evidential rationality is not the only mode of rationality. Pragmatically authorized beliefs are perfectly rational, albeit validated in the prudential rather than cognitive order of reasons.

Cognition has both its theoretical and its practical side, and we do well to give the former priority over the latter.

But the fact remains that we confront a complex goal structure that must be able to encompass various sorts of injunctions:

1. The *purely* cognitive: "Avoid accepting falsehoods."
2. The ethical: "Give people the benefit of doubt: think well of them insofar as possible."
3. The prudential: "When *nihil obstat,* accept what will demonstrably conduce to the realization of legitimate ends."

Within the framework of the overall cognitive project the first of these no doubt has *priority.* But that does not mean that the rest can simply be dismissed. Their disappearance can certainly not be effected by waving the magic wand of "rationality." For "Acceptance of *P* is rationally indicated" can be substantiated in very different directions: evidential, prudential, ethical, etc. The province of rationality is extensive—no one sector can simply expel the rest. We must acknowledge the multichromatic complexity of reason. (Compare Table 1.)

Table 1
The Taxonomy of Reason

Theoretical (Probative: Acceptance-Oriented) Reasoning
- *formal* (mathematics, logic, language, etc.)
- *evidential* (factual "inductive" reasoning in science and common life)

Practical (Pragmatic: Choice-Oriented) Reasoning
- *evaluative*
  - *axiological* (value-oriented)
    - geared to cognitive values
    - geared to affective values
    - geared to moral values
    - and so on
  - *prudential* (interest-oriented)
- *instrumental* ("value-free" means-ends reasoning)

*****

Let P be a proposition asserting the reality of a state of affairs that lies wholly outside one's control. And let us adopt the definition:

$A(P)$ = I accept that P.

With "acceptance" construed not so much in terms of belief as in terms of endorsement we shall here have something which indeed *does* lie within one's control.

Now $A(P)$ & $A(-P)$ can safely be eliminated on grounds of rationality. But for any proposition P the choice between $A(P)$ & $-A(-P)$ and $-A(P)$ & $A(-P)$ and $-A(P)$ & $-A(-P)$ remains available. How can one reasonably resolve this choice?

Consider the question of ranking the (preferability of) the following possibilities, which are mutually exclusive and exhaustive:

(1) $A(P)$ & $-A(-P)$ & P

(2) $A(P)$ & $-A(-P)$ & $-P$

(3) $-A(P)$ & $A(-P)$ & P

(4) $-A(P)$ & $A(-P)$ & $-P$

(5) $-A(P)$ & $-A(-P)$ & P

(6) $-A(P)$ & $-A(-P)$ & $-P$

Let us make two suppositions regarding the particular proposition P that is at issue:

1. If P is indeed true, then we shall sustain a big loss if our posture is wrong—that is, if $A(-P)$ and even if $-A(P)$. On the other hand, we would secure at least some gain by being right.

2. If $-P$, then it doesn't really make that much difference what we do: the gains or losses sustained in cases (2), (4), (6) are comparatively small relative to the loss we would incur in cases (3) and (5).

3. We gain by being completely right, as per (1).

Then we have the following situation with respect to the six aforelisted possibilities:

(1) a gain

(2) a small gain or loss

(3) a big loss

(4) a small gain or loss

(5) a big loss

(6) a small gain or loss

Since by choosing *A(P)* we can (for sure) avert the prospect of a big loss, this is, in the circumstances, the prudent and "reasonable" thing to do. Accepting *P* is prudentially indicated—unless, of course, contrary to present assumptions we had excellent reason to be confident that *-P*.

Something like this is clearly the way in which the decision theorist commited to a prudential approach to the matter would resolve the situation in a case of this sort. And this is exactly the consideration that Pascal sets out to exploit in the Wager argument.

The leading idea of modern decision theory (of which, after all, Pascal was the founder) is to treat the acceptance of theses as a *decision* that can quite appropriately be made in the light of practical considerations. For acceptance (assent, making up one's mind to endorse, etc.) is an act which, like other acts, is goal-oriented. And we have two closely related but yet distinguishable cognitive goals: the "purely" cognitive one of removing ignorance (having questions answered; obtaining information) and the more practical one of guiding action. Both sides of this divide, the theoretical and the practical, contribute to that overall goal structure of the cognitive enterprise in whose light the rationality of our management of our cognitive affairs must be appraised. We are dealing with a wider mode of rationality—one which, to be sure, sees action as rational in terms of benefit-optimization but takes the range of the potential benefits of even cognitive acts like acceptance to be larger than the limited sphere of specifically cognitive benefits.

Evidential considerations serve to indicate that a certain belief *is true*; pragmatic considerations serve to indicate that a certain belief *should be accepted as true*. Either produces essentially the same result—viz., that we are enjoined to accept something. But they lead to this common destination by significantly different routes.

On such an approach we will, of course, maintain rationality and only endorse beliefs "on the merits." But we recognize that *evidential* merit is not the only relevant kind—that there is also *pragmatic* merit. The objection that practical substantiation of a belief lacks probative efficacy in failing actually to *establish* its conclusion holds true enough. But it is beside the point. For the argument does not and is not designed to demonstrate or establish its conclusion as such; what it does do and is designed to do is to show that its acceptance is rationally indicated (in the specifically pragmatic mode of warrant). There is nothing whatever illicit or improper in traveling the pragmatic route. The impetus of both evidential and pragmatic indications is perfectly rational—in both circumstances we have good reason, though in the one case these reasons lie in the evidential and in the other in the practical sector.

*****

Pascal's perspective has it that if there is nothing clearly against it on the evidential (probative, confirmational) side, then it is rationally appropriate to allow oneself to be moved toward a thesis on the basis of such nonevidential considerations.[62] The rationale that underlies the Wager argument is of essentially this standard practical sort:

- Given one's commitment to certain (not inherently inappropriate) goals, the practice *C* is rationally indicated relative to these goals. (For example, given certain prudential goals of mine, a pious life is indicated.)

– Only if *P* is so does the practice *C* make sense. (Only if God exists does a pious life make sense.)

– On the evidential side there are no obstacles to the acceptance of *P*.

– Therefore: I am rationally required (relative to the goal in question) to accept *P*, because the presuppositions of a practice are rationally recommended by whatever recommends that practice as such).

What we have here is, in effect, an argument to the factual presuppositions or preconditions of a prudentially warranted practice. It is a "transcendental" argument (in the Kantian sense) from the pragmatic/prudential justification of a praxis to the pragmatic/prudential justification of the acceptance of the presuppositions or preconditions under which alone this practice makes sense (is rationally appropriate).

Whatever else may or may not be part of rationality, *prudence* is certainly a part of it. The rational man is (among other things) one who pursues his interests (his long-term real interests) as best he can discern them. Insofar as acceptance of certain theses conduces to this end, it is perfectly rational—at any rate insofar as the other demands of rationality (evidential rationality in particular) are not infringed thereby.

To grant extra-evidential considerations a role in forming our view of things is not a matter of doing violence to the evidence by selectively allowing some items to carry more weight than is their proper due. It is not a matter of *manipulating* the evidence at all, but rather of going beyond it, of *supplementing* the evidence, where insufficient, by recourse to other, nonevidential considerations. To take this line is not to distort the evidence, but to turn elsewhere when it leaves us in the lurch.

Someone might object: "Only the evidence should be allowed to count for rational acceptance." But why? What is the force of that "should"? In whose name does it speak?

Certainly not in the name of *rationality*—at any rate not a rationality broad enough to encompass our practical interests. For the interests of praxis go very much the other way, to the effect that in cases where we need guidance, we would do well to take it from any respectable source we can find.

The practical dimension of belief means that there is more at stake here than mere information. As William James argued with eloquence and clarity, these prudentially grounded beliefs can provide us a crucial impetus to effective action. It might be a long shot that my endurance will hold out until I reach the goal line. But once I abandon my belief that it will, failure is assured. The crucial rule of prudentially validated belief is to enable and encourage us to make the effort needed to attain inherently valuable goals.

The point is simply that rational commitment is multidimensional, and that "X is rationally committed to accepting *P*" can be cashed out in various directions—as many of them as there are good reasons, specifically including those of evidential justification, ethical justification, prudential justification, etc. And different *kinds* of constraints do not thereby cease to be constraints any more than different kinds of dogs thereby cease to be dogs. There is no more sense to saying that the prudential justification of beliefs is not *real* justification than there is in saying that Pomeranians aren't *real* dogs.

*****

Various thinkers drive a wedge between religious belief and reason. "Our most holy religion is founded in *faith*, not in reason," said David Hume, tongue in cheek,[63] and the names of theologians who agree with this contention are legion. But Pascal certainly does not belong to this "belief without reason" school of thought. His position is very different. It turns on recognizing the *complexity* of reason as a resource of broad scope that includes not merely probative (evidential/demonstrative) reason, but prudential reason, value-geared reason, and other modes as well.

The rational thing, as Locke and Hume tell it, is to proportion belief to the evidence. And so it is—in matters of pure theory. But man does not live by theory alone; there are also other interests: prudential, moral, and religious ones among them. We are not disembodied spectators off the world's stage, and more than mere information is at issue when we accept propositions. As war is too important to be left to the generals, so belief is too important to be left to the theoreticians. And just that is the key to Pascal's approach: that theorizing reason is not the only legitimate species of reason, and that the heart, too, has its *reasons.* Empiricist philosophers to the contrary notwithstanding, we must avoid equating reason with one single sector of its natural domain. The fundamental idea of probabilistic decision theory from Pascal onward is that we must deal in *expectations,* that both probabilities and utilities must be consulted in matters of acceptance, and that relatively improbable options may prevail if the cost-benefit situation is sufficiently favorable. With the realm of reason at large there are no compelling grounds why practical reason must keep silent where theoretical reason fails to speak.[64]

"To decide to cultivate belief in God when, epistemically, the odds are . . . against his existing . . . is deliberately to reject all rational principles of belief," thunders the atheist *ex cathedra.*[65] Stuff and nonsense! Opponents of Pascal's approach make things easy for themselves by equating rationality in general with *evidential* rationality. They then characterize acceptance on prudential grounds as an insult to reason that endorses irrational belief[66] and defaults on our moral obligation to the truth, since "if the belief has been accepted on insufficient evidence . . . it is sinful, because stolen in defiance of our duty to mankind."[67] But this equating of *rational* warrant with *evi-*

dential warrant is itself an attempt to gain by theft what can only be the fruit of arduous (and very problematic) philosophical labor.

To move from the unproblematic truism, "Rational belief must be based on compelling reasons" to the conclusion "Rational belief must be based on supportive evidence," we need the mediating premise: "Only evidence alone can provide reasons for accepting a thesis." But this thesis is available only if it can be shown that the sole cogently warranting reasons are evidential reasons—that rationally cogent compulsion can be had from no source save evidence alone, that man's intellectual interests are his only appropriate interests. This is certainly a *possible* contention, but it is no less certainly a far from *plausible* one. There is simply no warrant for confining good reasons for credence to the realm of evidence alone, simply excluding from the domain of rational warrant all reference to the practical, prudential, moral, etc. Well-evidenced information is not our sole (or even prime) object in life. As William James insisted, what we accept can crucially condition our capacity to realize great objects. Evidential rationality is not the only sort of rationality there is.

Pascal himself saw the matter in essentially this light. Placing one's bet on the side that God exists is, as Pascal sees it, the rational thing to do. But the rationality that it reflects is that of practical (pragmatic) reason rather than the evidential rationality of factual inquiry. It is the rationality of action rather than abstract speculation, of the demands of life rather than the demands of pure thought.

Consider the following objection:

> All that an argument along the lines of Pascal's Wager manages to do is to show that belief in God is warranted on prudential grounds—that such belief is in a way advantageous. But surely it is possible for a belief to be at once beneficial and false. The argumentation, even if successful, fails to demonstrate or establish that God actually exists.

It is sensible to absorb the impetus of this blow and to recognize and acknowledge just exactly this feature of the Wager argument as a pragmatic validation. Unlike evidential reasons for thesis acceptance, pragmatic reasons do not render their "conclusions" any more likely or probable or certain in evidential terms. They do not operate in the *evidential* dimension at all. Pragmatic reasons function outside the evidential sphere. Nevertheless, pragmatic reasons do put us into a position where we are justified—*pragmatically* justified—in accepting certain theses notwithstanding the fact that we cannot view them as probatively established by way of supporting evidence. What pragmatic reasons can accomplish is to show—in cases where evidential considerations leave the issue indecisively suspended *in terra incognita*—that we may nevertheless be thoroughly well-advised to accept the contentions at issue, because doing this effectively conduces to our aims and purposes. This is not so in the sense of "It would be nice if this thesis were true," but rather in that of "Since this thesis may well be true, for aught we know, it is advantageous that we should 'hedge our bets' in its direction."

It may seem tempting to say: "Where evidential reason fails to resolve an issue, there can be no real justification for coming down on one side or the other at all; a skeptical suspension of judgment is the best, the only appropriate course here." But this, of course, is simply not so. From the fact that a given thesis is not established evidentially it nowise follows that it cannot be justified at all. For the ground rules for *evidential* reason do not (and need not) apply entire and unchanged on the side of *practical* reason.

Some may perhaps insist: "Where rational acceptance is concerned, only purely cognitive benefits can be allowed to count—any other sort of 'benefits' must be put aside." But why should this be so? What, after all, is the point of thesis acceptance? We ask questions, conduct inquiry, and accept theses not *only* for "purely theoretical" purposes—to extend our information, period—but also to guide our actions, to orient us physically and psychologically in the world on which we have been placed. The aims of inquiry are only partly intellectual; they are substiantially practical as well: we have a stake in information, to be sure, but also in many other goods. The utilities of the corpus of our beliefs are complex, its benefits diverse: not only purely informational but practical as well. There is no good reason why the legitimation of thesis acceptance should be restricted to one sector of this domain.

*****

The pragmatic approach to belief validation envisions the teleology of belief as a compound, with both a probative/evidential and a pragmatic/prudential dimension. And it concedes a definite priority here: a sequential ordering of evidence first and prudence second. As far as belief is concerned, considerations of pragmatic interest do not enter in until after considerations of evidence have been given their due. Pragmatic validation cannot properly be used to invalidate our evidentially grounded beliefs but only to supplement them: If we know that we cannot leap the chasm, then "there's no use fooling ourselves."[68]

Accordingly, prudential considerations do not appropriately come into play in such cases until evidential considerations have done their work. If the factual evidence countervails, that's that. To maintain the rational proprieties, our practically warranted beliefs must never *conflict* with those that are warranted on evidential grounds. It will not do to say: "Let interest override evidence."[69] But there is no comparable problem about saying: "Let interest speak where evidence is silent." "Do not believe *contrary* to the evidence: always correct your beliefs in the light of evidence" is a perfectly reasonable and appropriate injunction. "Do not believe *beyond* the explicit assurances of the evidence" is not.[70] No doubt, in those situations where the voice of evidence speaks audibly, it must be heeded. Pragmatic considerations can be used to *supplement* evidentially secured information but not to *countermand* it: they can prevail against ignorance, but not against facts.[71] To fly in the face of validated fact is patently inappropriate, and even to go against merely well-evidenced fact is problematic. But where there is no question of this—where *gap-filling* is at issue because the voice of evidence is silent or too low for audibility—indulging the demands of prudence is perfectly legitimate.

With Pascal the issue is certainly not *simply* one of the pragmatic benefits of a belief—of the man who simply "has to" believe his wife faithful and his friend trustworthy, lest he himself be destroyed by disillusionment. For there may well be decisive counterevidence to which one cannot reasonably shut one's eyes. What is at issue in the case now in view is a matter of *transcending* the evidence, not one of ignoring, let alone *violating,* it.

Evidentially validated fact deserves primacy throughout the range of rational belief. But that does not mean that it exhausts the domain. It is certainly not the case that "where evidence is silent, no other cognitive interest can properly speak." It is one thing to let pragmatic reasons *countermand* evidential considerations and another to let them provide supplements—to use practical reason to validate propositions in areas where inquiring or "theoretical" reason cannot reach.

In taking this route we can, of course, claim no more than to have resolved the issue for all *practical* purposes. But there is no reason why we cannot or should not do this, as long as we do not delude ourselves into thinking that we have done something other than what we have—viz., prudentially justifiable gap-filling. As long as we avoid the deceptive step of passing off a prudentially based claim as cognitively based, we are not getting involved in a delusion or confusion.

Good reasons for belief can certainly be found outside the evidential domain, for pragmatic reasons are not less *reasons* than evidential ones. And yet we are told: "Every time we let ourselves believe for unworthy reasons, we weaken our power of self-control, of doubting, of judicially and fairly weighing evidence."[72] Rubbish! (1) For one thing, who is to say that nonevidential reasons are *ipso facto* unworthy? (2) For another, why need recourse to nonevidential reasons weaken our power for weighing evidence any more than recourse to fruit weaken our power for digesting vegetables?

Even in the case of purely cognitive situations there are sanctions on indecision and suspension of judgment. For man is an inquiring animal (*homo quaerens*)—he wants and needs answers to his questions. Ignorance and indecision exact a toll in terms of discomfort and disorientation. For both theoretical and practical reasons we want and need answers to our questions—to satisfy our questioning mind or to guide our actions in the light of accepted beliefs. Man's need for achieving a cognitive orientation in the world is every bit as crucial as his need for food, shelter, or clothing.

2. Different Realms of Truth?

It must be stressed that different routes to acceptance (the evidential, the practical, the moral, and perhaps others) do not lead to different realms of truth—to different spheres of fact or different worlds. We need not become Averroists and adopt the idea of multiple (and potentially discordant) realms of truth. Though different sorts of considerations may inspire us toward accepting various claims, those claims themselves will lie in one self-same plane of factuality. We are concerned with the shaping of one integrated body of knowledge, admission to which can be gained by different routes—the evidential, the practical, etc. (That is why we are not prepared to pit pragmatic reasons for acceptance against evidential ones, and confine pragmatic validation to the role of cognitive gap-filling.)

Consider the situation adduced by William James:

> Suppose . . . I am climbing in the Alps, and have had the ill-luck to work myself into a position from which the only escape is by a terrible leap. Being without similar experience, I have no evidence of my ability to perform it successfully; but hope and confidence in myself make me sure I shall not miss my aim and nerve my feet to execute what without those subjective emotions would perhaps have been impossible. But suppose that, on the contrary, the emotions of fear and mistrust preponderate; or suppose that, having just read the *Ethics of Belief* [by W. K. Clifford], I feel it would be sinful to act upon an assumption unverified by previous experience,—why, then I shall hesitate so long that at last, exhausted and trembling, and launching myself in a moment of despair, I miss my foothold and roll into the abyss.[73]

My pragmatic belief that "I can do it" presumably has to be a *real* belief, a full-fledged fact-purporting conviction of my ability to accomplish the task.

To be sure, there are indeed variant modes of "acceptance" that differ from the acceptance-as-true at issue with actual beliefs—acceptance as an assumption, for example, or as a working hypothesis, or as a rule of procedure (to be followed "as if" I believed it, while actually suspending judgment or even disbelieving). But this sort of thing is not at issue with pragmatically based acceptance. Here we deal not with such qualified modes of "acceptance," but with the outright *acceptance* at issue in what we endorse as true. Proceeding in the spirit of a "working assumption" along the lines of "Well, I've got nothing to lose, so let's go ahead and try" would in general be something very different. For basing its acceptance on pragmatic grounds, we are nevertheless *accepting* a thesis (pure and simple), giving it credence and using it as an element of the mental map we draw to orient ourselves in the world's scheme of things. Action "as if" something is true stops well short of actual belief, because beliefs are the materials of our information (or *purported* information) as to how matters stand. In entering the sphere of working hypotheses and assumptions we step away from actual belief and thus lose the crucial prospect of proceeding with real conviction.

But can pragmatically based acceptances ever be as rationally firm and as solid as acceptance that is evidentially based? That depends on how we construe rational legitimation. With respect to *evidential* rationality the answer is of course No. But with respect to *prudential* rationality it can certainly be Yes. In the context of this question we must once more stress the multisidedness of "rationality."

*****

Consider the following objection:

> Only evidentially based belief can possibly be legitimate. Pragmatic considerations can at most warrant *action* (on an as-if basis). They should never be allowed to succeed in validating *acceptance* of a belief.

This is surely incorrect. To let one's actions say one thing where one's actual beliefs say something else is *hypocrisy.* And while hypocrisy may be the homage vice pays to virtue, it nevertheless stands on the side of vice. Acting "as if" a thesis were true is an emphatic and public form of endorsement. To do this *systematically,* while privately withholding credence, not only is unreasonable: it is morally reprehensible. Rationality calls for aligning one's actions to one's beliefs; morality for aligning one's beliefs to one's actions. For persons of moral integrity "actions speak louder than words." Once we admit that pragmatic considerations can appropriately dictate action, we must be prepared to concede that they can dictate belief as well.

Pascal's Wager argument addresses itself to the issue of the *warrant for belief.* It is not a matter of simply and only recommending a certain course of action (even one which, if followed, will probably engender belief). Leibniz was quite wrong in this regard when he objected:

> This argument shows nothing about what one ought to believe, but only about how one ought to act. That is to say, it proves only that those who do not believe in God should act as if they did. [74]

What the Wager argument actually shows is that it is *belief* that is rationally warranted and not mere action "as if" one believed. It is (presumably) genuine religiosity that the deity sets as a precondition for bestowing those benefits which the argument contemplates. (An omniscient deity is of course clever enough to distinguish this from mere surface conformity.) The argument is concerned not with belief as such, but with the rational warrant for it. Leibniz uncharacteristically missed the subtlety of Pascal's reasoning, which is concerned to find a *via media* between actually establishing the belief at issue to be true and merely recommending action as if it were true.

Pascal's Wager does not address itself to "degrees of belief." It does not turn on some such scale as

(1) mere *nominal acceptance* as tantamount to acting as though *P* were true,

(2) *pragmatic acceptance* as tantamount to treating *p* as true—perhaps without actual belief,

(3) *belief* as tantamount to actual endorsement of *P*—which may yet be hesitant or subject to reservation,

(4) *genuine conviction* as tantamount to being "fully and completely persuaded" that *P* is true.

It is not with such psychological and/or epistemological endorsement that Pascal's Wager is concerned, but with the issue of *rational warrant*—with the question would it be reasonable (justifiable) to accept that *P*.

Of course, someone might wonder just exactly where theism does stand evidentially—just how *probable* it is in the existing evidential state of things that God exists. But Pascal would reply that such a person is barking up the wrong tree—that this inquiry is apologetically fruitless. (As Pascal sees it, the nonbeliever is in as poor a position to make effective use of theological evidence as the person uninitiated into a language can interpret the evidence of his ears, which is, in fact, just as likely to confuse as to inform.) It is not that there is something wrong with demonstration, but just that it cannot begin to do the job that needs to be done in apologetics. The crucial fact here is that evidential considerations do not decide the issue but leave it "up in the air," veiled in the obscurity of an information gap.

3. Is Acceptance on Prudential Grounds Irrational?

Once one acknowledges that prudential grounds can provide a rational warrant for action, there is no obstacle to having them warrant that particular sort of "cognitive act" involved in the acceptance of a certain contention.

Yet is it not rationally inappropriate to let acceptance and belief outrun the reach of actual evidence? Is the acceptance on prudential grounds not something inherently irrational?

But why on earth should it be? In general it is (quintessentially) rational to follow the dictates of prudence—to act on that alternative which seems optimally advantageous. (Indeed that is how economists and decision theorists *define* "rationality.") And if this is so with actions in general, then why not in the particular case of "acts of *acceptance*"? Throughout the sphere of rational decision, acceptance is a matter of combining and mixing considerations of probability (evidence) and utility (value). So why not in this sphere of propositional acceptance as well? If it is in general rationally appropriate—indeed wise—to follow the dictates of prudence, then why not also in this matter of belief? After all, a prudential reason is a perfectly good reason.

Consider the following objection:

> [To accept something for pragmatic reasons] is to advocate wishful thinking. . . . The crux precisely is that appeal is being made to desires of some sort, and not to . . . reasons as grounds.[75]

This is quite false. A doctrine of practical rationality continues to appeal to "reasons as grounds," but to *prudential* rather than *evidential* reasons. It does not abandon the "principles of rationality" to the effect that beliefs should be adopted only for good reasons; it simply stresses the breadth of the idea of "good reason" as a conception that covers both evidential and prudential reasons. To insist that such prudential pragmatic reasons are by nature unable to justify acts of acceptance is either to deny that they can justify *any* acts, which seems very strange, or else specifically to remove acts of acceptance from their purview, which needs a supportive argument that has never yet been provided. What is sauce for the goose of praxis in general is surely also sauce for the gander of our specifically *cognitive* praxis.

*****

But exactly what is the epistemic status of a pragmatically warranted belief? Clearly it is not that of an item of *secured knowledge,* something whose truth has been established or otherwise less strongly substantiated through evidential backing. From a strictly epistemic standpoint its status is no more than that of a rationally warranted presumption validated as a matter of evidential gap-filling in a situation of practical import. But, of course, its acceptance does thereby obtain a degree of rational warrant—a warrant, to be sure, operative on the practical (rather than evidential) side.

Does such endorsement on pragmatic grounds represent a defect in rationality? Is it not irrational to accept something as true if we do not "know" it to be so—that is, if we do not have conclusive evidence? No—it is not irrational; it may be perfectly rational, although *pragmatically* rational. As William James insisted, it is quintessentially the task of rationality to harmonize the demands of our human nature with the realities of our environing world as best we can determine them. The pragmatic legitimation of belief is simply an aspect of this general program.

The justificatory reasoning at work here is itself prudential. It argues that it is altogether defensible and legitimate to fill an evidential void by prudential means, but here defensible means "*prudentially* defensible." To accept a thesis on suitably developed prudential grounds is perfectly rational, but a thesis supported by a structure of rationality that is based on prudence. Such "prudential enabling beliefs" are (*ex hypothesi*) not probatively constrained by purely cognitive/epistemic considerations. But they are certainly not irrational. They are unproblematically warranted as "reasonable" and "justified" but of course are so in the prudential order: they are perfectly reasonable—but "reasonable" in a sense that allows pragmatic considerations to play a role.

Someone may object:

> Once you accept claims on other than evidential grounds alone—once you allow considerations other than the purely evidential to influence your beliefs—are you not opening the door to the "Ministry of Truth" of George Orwell's *1984*; paving the way for beliefs motivated by the pursuit of personal profit or political expediency?[76]

But this is hardly a sensible objection. It is like saying "Once you use your motor car for reasons other than going to work, are you not paving the way to chasing loose women and transporting stolen goods?" To allow practical interests to play a role in determining our beliefs in certain circumstances is scarcely to throw all cognitive caution to the winds—if only because we have a pervasive and paramount interest in the securing of accurate information. The fact that a resource can be misused is no good reason for not using it at all.

*****

Again, consider the following objection to any form of Pascal-like argumentation:

> You distinguish beneficial (prudential/pragmatic) reasons for belief from evidential ones. But surely "It is beneficial to believe that *P*" does not entail "*P* is actually (nor even *probably*) the case." It might well be beneficial to believe something (e.g., that God exists) even if this is not so at all. Surely this sort of argumentation will not be probatively cogent.

This objection is (in its way) right. But it is also irrelevant. For the line of justificatory reasoning at issue in Pascal's Wager argument does not take the form:

– It is beneficial to believe that God exists.

–*Therefore*: God (probably) exists.

which is certainly not cogent in its highly problematic mixing of beneficial and factual contentions. Rather, the argument takes the form

– It is beneficial to believe that God exists.

– The available evidence does not countervail against the belief, nor do other legitimate interests stand in the way.

– *Therefore*: We are rationally warranted (in the pragmatic mode of warrant) to believe that God exists.

The step of moving from this conclusion to an endorsement of "God exists" is not an *inferential* step, but a *practical* one. In taking this step we come to be committed to the initial argument's conclusion all right, but not on its basis. Its invalidity becomes irrelevant.

One recent writer objects that Pascal's argument does not make it reasonable to become a religious person, for while it equips us with a *motive*, it does not provide a *reason*:

> [I] t is not the belief in an infinite gain which makes it reasonable to be religious. I may get it into my head that setting fire to the bus station will get me into heaven, but this does not make it reasonable for me to perform this "religious act."[77]

This observation is perfectly correct but misfires as an objection to Pascal. Obviously if I aim at end *E* and believe that act *A* is a necessary condition for its attainment, it will nevertheless be reasonable for me to do *A* only if this belief of mine (viz., that *A* is a condition for *E*) is itself reasonable.[78] In the bus station example it clearly is not. But with Pascal's Wager there is no difficulty here. For the pivotal connection at issue (viz., that the Christian God, should he exist, will reward belief) must be deemed unproblematic in the light of the God concept we must suppose the addressees of the argument to hold.

The salient point is that the existence of a cogent *motive* for having a belief can, in the absence of evidential impediment, constitute a perfectly sound *reason* for adopting it—albeit a reason in the prudential rather than evidential order of deliberations.

*****

In the final analysis there is no conflict between *theoria* and *praxis* in this area of rational belief. Our interest in *theoria* is deeply practical—we are the creature that must make its evolutionary way in the world by its wits. Evidential considerations are themselves underpinned and legitimated by practical considerations. Theory and practice form a seamless whole in the domain of inquiry. At the deepest level there is no opposition here, but rather a coordination that assigns to each party its proper role in a mutually beneficial collaboration.

4. The Charges of Self-Deception and Wishful Thinking

Self-deception takes place when one knows something (or is so circumstanced that one really *ought* to know it) but nevertheless either fails to recognize it or persists in believing something incompatible with it. It is a matter of refusing to face the plain and patent facts.[79] Is this sort of thing at issue in Pascal?

Critics incline to say that "The main irrationality of religion is preferring comfort to truth."[80] But *this* is certainly not Pascal's way. Were the nonexistence of God a demonstrable truth, Pascal would certainly not urge belief upon us. As he sees it, it is precisely because the issue is one that lies beyond the range of evidential reason that there is room for faith. His skepticism is no mere ornament; it is the very foundation of his enterprise. If the nonexistence of God were a plain and patent fact, Pascal's Wager would indeed be a matter of self-deception. But to claim that this is so is not simply a matter of criticizing Pascal; it is a matter of begging the question on the side of atheism—of dishing theism by simple fiat.

Pascal does not take the "I believe it because I want to" line of his later compatriot Pierre Jurieu: *Je le crois parce que je veux le croire.*[81] For one thing, he does not think that the will can control belief. For another, he does not think it reasonable to accept something solely and wholly on the basis of inclination. He does not want to sever the linkage of (rational) belief to reason, but simply to broaden the range of "reason" to include practical reason as well.

Social scientists and cognitive psychologists occasionally ruminate on the benefits of self-deception and the usefulness of false beliefs.[82] For example, one recent textbook has it that:

> People sometimes may require overly optimistic or overly pessimistic subjective probabilities to goad them to effective action. . . . Thus it is far from clear that a bride or groom would be well advised to believe, on their wedding day, that the probability of their divorce is as high as .40. A baseball player with an average of .200 may not be best served, as he steps up to bat, to believe that the probability that he will get a hit is only .2. . . . We probably would have few novelists, actors, or scientists if all potential applicants to these careers took action based on a normatively justifiable probability of success.[83]

There are, no doubt, various situations in life where beliefs that could and should be recognized as false by an agent (which is not necessarily the case with these probabilistic examples!) might nevertheless be beneficial for his conduct of affairs. Yet this sort of thing is emphatically *not* at issue with Pascal's Wager. To hold that the belief at issue is one that "could or should be recognized as false" prejudices the case totally.

Just here is where Pascal's skepticism comes in—his contention that inquiring reason cannot settle the matter and that from the purely *evidential* point of view the question is occluded by a fog of ignorance. Be self-deception beneficial or not, it is not something that Pascal endorses.

To blunt the charge of self-deception against Pascal's Wager, we need to step back and take a realistic view of exactly what an argument of this sort sets out to accomplish. It militates prudentially toward acceptance of (the truth of) a certain theological thesis *P*: to render *P* acceptable on *prudential grounds.* It certainly does not seek to prove the truth of *P*, and we would gravely misrepresent what it does if we say that, now that the argument is in hand, we have *established* that *P.* But we can certainly (rationally) endorse *P* on its basis, thus claiming that *P* is true—though we must view the rationale of this claim as having the nature of a *hope* rather than a *fait établi.* The pragmatic recourse to hope and faith, avowed explicitly, should serve to undermine the basis on which many objections to Pascal's argumentation are predicated.

*****

But "self-deception" is one thing and "wishful thinking" another.[84] And so we must also confront, on Pascal's behalf, the objection that to allow prudential considerations to guide belief is not more than "wishful thinking," predicated on the overly optimistic idea that reality is congenial to our human interests. This objection overlooks the deep analogy between the *inductive* and the *pragmatic* situation, in both of which we are constrained to leap beyond the content of the evidence on hand. Induction is inference to the best explanation (the optimal systematization of our established and conjectured information).[85] Practical reasoning is inference to the best plan of action, the optimal *modus operandi*—including its cognitive ramifications. It is no more "wishful thinking," no worse a "lapse from strict rationality," to let *practical* reasoning indicate that matters stand in a way that optimizes our *behavioral* commitments than to let *inductive* reasoning indicate that matters stand in a way that optimizes our *cognitive* commitments.

A sound practical argument that a certain belief is well-advised is compatible with the falsity of its conclusion, with being mistaken in the substance of one's belief. Would acceptance of a belief on the basis of such a probatively inconclusive argument not diminish the rationality of man?

By no means. There once again stands before us the Humean reminder (indeed the lesson of the skeptical tradition in general) that sound inductive arguments also never yield more than potentially false conclusions which, despite that fact, deserve acceptance. ("There is adequate evidence for accepting *P*" invariably fails to yield "*P* is true."[86]) Induction—inference to the best systematization—is just as much (or little) a matter of "wishful thinking" as is the sort of inference to an optimizing presupposition that is at issue in the acknowledgment of prudential reasons.

Yet the charge of irrationalism still remains to be dealt with. Consider the following objection:

> Acceptance on nonevidential, pragmatic grounds is rationally unwarranted. For in the absence of (suitably definitive) evidence one does not really *know* that the thesis at issue is indeed true. It is little more than self-deception to deem oneself entitled to make truth-claims in such cases.

The appropriate response here calls for a closer look at the key words "warranted" and "entitled." For we indeed *are* warranted and entitled, but pragmatically not evidentially. And pragmatic reasons are perfectly good reasons. As long as we do not deceive ourselves as to the basis of our claims, our acceptance of them is perfectly appropriate—and fully justified. There is nothing improper or inappropriate about making a pragmatically grounded truth-claim as long as we do not mistake its character and misrepresent its basis to ourselves or to others. As long as we recognize what we are doing for what it is—as long as we are candid and do not present the situation as different from what it is—there is nothing inappropriate about adopting a belief for nonevidential reasons. Belief is perfectly warranted in these circumstances, albeit in the practical rather than evidential mode of warrant.

5. Is Acceptance on Prudential Grounds Immoral?

It is sometimes said that evidence alone ought to guide belief, not interest. But what is the nature of this "ought"?

In his classic 1877 essay on "The Ethics of Belief" (to which William James's even more famous 1895 essay on "The Will to Believe" offered a reply), the English philosopher W. K. Clifford maintained his famous thesis that:

> [I]t is wrong always, everywhere, and for anyone, to believe anything upon insufficient evidence.[87]

It is clear that a great deal will turn on just how Clifford's words are construed here. If "wrong" were altered to "risky," the thesis would become an unproblematic platitude. For presumably that is exactly what we mean by speaking of literally "*insufficient* evidence"—evidence that leaves open the prospect that matters may possibly go wrong. But given this replacement, the thesis would no longer bear the moral overtones which Clifford unquestionably intended it to have—as is shown by his talk of "duties" and of "guilt" in this connection.

A claim to knowledge undoubtedly requires an entitlement-to-assent—a "right to be sure." But the entitlement at issue is not a *right* in the specifically moral sense of the term. For the obligation to be rational is not a *moral* obligation, and lapses from cognitive rationality are not—in general—*moral* lapses. The sanctions of erroneous cognition are not those of *morality* but those of *prudence*—of losing out on these goods inherent in getting at the truth of things. The goals relevantly operative in the cognitive sphere relate not to our moral ends but to our prudential means in the proper management of rational inquiry, exposition, discussion, and argumentation.

The rules of ethics and morality are correlative with the purpose of avoiding damage to the rights and interests of others. By contrast, the person who violates the epistemic standards of cognitive rationality simply manages to reason badly and thereby (in general) damages no one but himself. In failing to be rational one does not violate the valid claims of others but rather frustrates one's own cognitive objectives of getting at the truth of things (and presumably his practical objectives of successful goal-realization as well). The irrationality at issue is a matter not of *immorality,* but one of *imprudence*—of comporting oneself so as to impede the very objectives (theoretical and practical alike) that govern the cognitive enterprise on which one is engaged. Clifford's ethico-moral interpretation of belief must be rejected. It would thus be ill-advised to condemn Pascal's recourse to prudence on specifically *ethical* grounds.

As William James quite properly argued against Clifford, the enterprise of inquiry is governed not only by the negative injunction "Avoid error!" but no less importantly by the positive injunction "Achieve truth!"[88] And in the domain of objective fact—where it is inevitable that the assertive *content* of our claims will outstrip the information we can ever gather by way of supportive *evidence* for them—this goal of achieving truth inevitably and unavoidably involves some risk of error. There is nothing irrational—let alone *wrong*—about accepting this risk.

Moral condemnation wholly aside, there are serious problems for this doctrine that it is wrong to accept anything that has some tincture of evidence-transcendence about it. Clifford's position is ultimately indefensible—as James rightly emphasized—partly because of its tendency to stifle action (because rational action must be aligned with reasonable belief), partly because it stultifies knowledge (since its unrealistically rigoristic view of the justification of knowledge-claims engenders utter skepticism).

The James-Clifford controversy conveys an important lesson for epistemology. It constrains us to recognize that as regards this matter of knowledge (as in other ways) we live in an imperfect world. The ultimate ideal of absolute perfection is outside our grasp: the prospect of averting all risk of error is not attainable in this epistemic dispensation. Outside the substantively contentless arena of formal reasoning in logic and mathematics we have no route to the truth that is not in some degree "chancy." Gambling with the truth is simply part of the human condition.[89]

*****

We are told that:

> Many would consider that it is highly immoral to choose to believe propositions . . . when the evidence is now known not to support them.[90]

But two issues should give these "many" pause: (1) Is the believer flying in the face of the evidence or is the evidence merely insufficient—is there positive evidence in hand that is actually *counterindicative*, or is evidence merely lacking, simply silent on the issue? (2) What is the believer's reason for failing to be guided by the evidence alone—is it something inherently creditable (e.g., a reluctance to think ill of a friend), or is it discreditable (e.g., a reluctance to think well of an enemy)? Surely if questions of this sort are resolved favorably—if the belief does not actually violate the evidence and if it has the backing of an ethically neutral or even creditable rationale—then there is no good reason for bringing the heavy guns of morality to bear and condemn those evidence-overreaching believers on *moral* grounds. The person who gives others the benefit of doubt—who thinks well of them in the absence of counter-evidence and does not insist on positive evidence for this step—is doing something not morally reprehensible, but the very reverse. To repeat: evidential rationality is not the only rationality there is.

There indeed is an ethics of belief, and various precepts regarding belief are part of it. (For example: "Believe the best of people that the circumstances admit of.") But the Cliffordian precept "Believe only that for which you have a solid basis of evidence" is not one of them. (If it were, whence would one get the evidence itself?) As James insisted: "a rule of thinking which would absolutely prevent me from acknowledging certain kinds of truth if those kinds of truth were really there, would be an irrational rule."[91] Cognition and economic life are analogous: only if we are willing to extend some degree of credit to a cognitive faculty or resource can we determine if it is indeed creditworthy. James was surely right: if we want to engage in the cognitive enterprise of empirical inquiry—if we want to obtain answers to our questions about the world—we have no choice but to accept a risk of error. The science that is not prepared to have future science amend or reject its declarations has no alternative but to keep silent. In this cognitive domain risk is something we cannot evade, however ardently (and sensibly) we may strive to reduce its magnitude. Only by being willing to run in the race do we stand a chance—however slim—of winning it. "Nothing ventured, nothing gained." Even as risk-running is unavoidable in life in general, so running a risk of error is an unavoidable requisite of the cognitive life.[92] And just here is the nerve of Pascal's reasoning. Life is a risky business. Its intelligent conduct calls for a mechanism for rational decision-making. But once we have such a mechanism, there is no good reason for excluding matters of religion from its preview. One pivotal lesson of Pascal's Wager argument is surely this, that rationality in thought and in action are parts of a seamless whole.

III
Practical Reasoning in Theology

1. God and Human Ignorance

This chapter will examine some issues of philosophical theology from the vantage point of decision theory and especially of the theory of games. Pouring old wine into such new bottles, it will endeavor to throw light both on the substance and on the spirit of Pascal's Wager argument.

Let us approach the matter of the existence of God from the angle of the question: What does Reality have in store for us? Specifically, does it have a God up its sleeves? And let us view this issue as reflecting a sort of game between Man and Reality. Man has two moves: to believe (*B*) or not to believe (*-B*) in God. And there are two possibilities for Reality: to afford the existence of God (*E*) or not (*-E*). Thus four states of affairs can in theory obtain:

	Man	*Reality*
(1)	*B*	*E*
(2)	*B*	*-E*
(3)	*-B*	*E*
(4)	*-B*	*-E*

Within the framework of present concerns we may suppose that the Man at issue is something of a doubter—

l'homme moyen sceptique who would prefer the comfortable and convenient posture of an undisturbed unbelief. This skeptically inclined man undoubtedly has a preferential stance toward the four alternatives. Thus (4) may be assumed to be his first preference. (While he would presumably fare better if *B* & *E* indeed obtained, we will suppose that Man is just willful or perverse enough to prefer -*B* "if the terms are right"—that is, if -*E*.) To be sure, if Man is indeed to believe, then he would obviously like to be right, so that (1) is preferable to (2). And (3) would clearly be the worst situation from Man's standpoint, since here he is not only wrong, but wrong in a way that foregoes benefits and poses dangers. Man's preferential ordering across the whole spectrum of possibilities accordingly emerges as -*B* & -*E*, *B* & *E*, *B* & -*E*, -*B* & *E*. His overall preference schedule thus stands at:

B & *E*	2
B & -*E*	3
-*B* & *E*	4
-*B* & -*E*	1

The resultant situation can thus be depicted as follows:

Reality's alternatives / *Man's choices*	*E*	-*E*
B	2	3
-*B*	4	1

In this situation Man has no dominant alternative in his "game against reality"—no one choice that will prove superior regardless of how matters actually stand. (Neither row outranks the other seriatim.) On orthodox decision-theoretic principles the prudent step for Man is accordingly to "play safe" by opting for the minimum-maximizing ("maximin") choice—namely *B*—a choice which will, at any rate, avert the prospect of worst coming to worst.

To be sure, one of nature's atheists who feels certain of -*E* will unhesitatingly opt for -*B*. But someone who is genuinely uncertain—who cannot even get a firm grip on the numerical probability of reality's alternatives—would plausibly be tempted by prudence to play safe at *B*. This line of consideration highlights the relation between skepticism and theism in deliberations of this sort. It is precisely because he cannot attain probabilistic assurance (let alone absolute certainty!) that Pascal's prudentially self-interested agnostic is led to belief as a "play safe" resolution in the setting of the Wager argument. As Pascal saw it, the prudent man is impelled to belief not by knowledge but by ignorance.

2. God and Human Wickedness

On the standard conception of the matter God's nature is (*ex hypothesi*) characterized by the three great omni's of traditional theology: he is omnipotent = all-powerful, omniscient = all-knowing, and omnibenevolent = all-good. But how can the world's *imperfection* possibly be reconciled with this? Specifically, how could such a God (if indeed real) possibly create a world in which human wickedness, the "moral evil" of traditional theology, is so prominent a feature?

We cannot say that God did not foresee the proliferation of human wickedness—his postulated omniscience clearly blocks this. Nor can we say that he is indifferent to man's wickedness to man—omnibenevolence precludes this. Nor, again, can we say that he is unable to prevent evil-doing—omnipotence stands in the way. How, then, can we explain it?

In the final analysis the explanation would have to take

the line that God is *unwilling* to prevent it—that its prevention would, as he sees it, exact an unacceptable price somewhere along the line. But how can this be?

We must suppose that God has various desiderata in view in his relation to man. He certainly wants man to believe in him—to acknowledge him and to love and trust him—but let this be put aside for the moment. And he certainly wants man to be good, to act in a kind, humane, trusting, generous, caring, and moral way. (This, of course, is simply an aspect of his own benevolent care that all should be well in the world.) No less importantly, however, God would undoubtedly want man to be *independent.* He would not want to force man's hand, to make him a mere puppet, but would want him to be an autonomous power, a free agent. Man is to be a creature, yes, but a creature with a will of its own capable of acting on its own initiative—with encouragement, to be sure, but without outright constraint or blatant intimidation. Wanting man to be good, God would not want to realize this positive end by negative means: by force, constraint, or "undue influence." For him, as for us, bad means can contaminate a good end. Accordingly, he must be prepared to let one desideratum, man's independence, take precedence over the other, man's goodness.

God's preferential-ranking of the relevant alternatives would thus presumably stand as follows:

God's choice	*Man's response*	*God's preferential rating*
independence	goodness	1
independence	wickedness	2
constraint	goodness	3
constraint	wickedness	(case impossible)

Since recourse to constraint automatically leads to God's *least* preferred alternative, he must opt for independence and "let things take their course." Even though human wickedness results (as he can perfectly well foresee), God would presumably see this outcome as superior to its alternatives, relative to his own scheme of values. (A world of disobedient men still is better than one of mere puppets.)

It is helpful to view God's stance toward man's wickedness in the perspective of a game situation. God has two moves: to trust man to do right or not to trust him (*T* or *-T*). Man has two moves: to be obedient to God's will or not (*W* or *-W*). Four possibilities are thus available: *T* & *W*, *T* & *-W*, *-T* & *W*, *-T* & *-W*.

We may suppose that man would want God to trust him and yet would nevertheless willfully prefer to meet trust with disobedience (thus preferring *T* & *-W* to *T* & *W*). God, for his part, also prefers to trust man but of course wants man to be obedient to his will (thus preferring *T* & *W* to *T* & *-W*). We thus arrive at the following preference schedules:

	God	*Man*	*God's preference rating*	*Man's preference rating*
(1)	*T*	*W*	1	2
(2)	*T*	*-W*	2	1
(3)	*-T*	*W*	3-or 4	3-or-4
(4)	*-T*	*-W*	3-or-4	3-or-4

This state of affairs engenders the following game situation:

God's choices / *Man's choices*	*T*	*-T*
W	2/1	3-or-4/3-or-4
-W	1/2	3-or-4/3-or-4

For God *T* dominates here. Man, realizing this circumstance, would presumably take advantage of it to opt for *-W*, with a result which, for God, is not better than second best. Yet even realizing this, God (if conceived along the indicated lines) remains locked in place at *T* by his own value structure.

To say that man's actions are not *predetermined* (constrained) by God is not of course to say that they cannot be *foretold* by him. Creation is an *enabling* action. Without it there are no actual eventuations at all in the contingent domain, but only possibilities. But with it there comes into being a reality which—in view of man's freedom of will—may or may not accord with God's own preferences. Given foreknowledge, God does not really take a chance—he runs no real risks. But he is nevertheless in a position where he "does not have it all his way" but must subordinate his abstract preferences regarding *results* (viz., his desire for man's goodness) to higher priorities regarding *process* (viz., man's freedom). In a wider sense God does indeed "get what he wants," but in a narrower sense (as depicted in the preceding game) he must settle for second best.

3. The Relation of God to Man

Consider how the question of man's faith in him might look from God's point of view. Should he interfere by intervening in the world's developments through revealing himself to encourage man's faith and obedience—or should he simply let matters take their course?

From God's own point of view certain specifiable preferences will clearly obtain. Other things being equal, he would doubtless wish not to intervene. God will not so manifest himself as to force our hand—to diminish the element of free and responsible choice involved in our turning to him. Clearly, a repeated and unambiguous, public, and overwhelming manifestation of divine action on the model of various Old Testament episodes would impinge on human freedom. As Pascal wrote to Mlle. de Roannez, "God would rather move the will than the intellect." Religious belief cannot—and *should* not!—be forced on the reluctant mind by constraints of reason alone. That is why the signals God sends us are mixed and not entirely unambiguous. As Pascal puts it: "If there were only one religion, God would be clearly manifest. And if there were no martyrs save in one religion, God would likewise be manifest. God being thus hidden, any religion which does not say that God is hidden is not true, and any religion which does not explain why does not instruct."[93] Thus God certainly prefers to remain "a hidden God" (*Deus absconditus*)[94] and would ideally have man believe even without revelation. But he very much does want man to believe and is willing to reveal himself if this is necessary to encourage belief. A lack of belief on man's part encouraged by God's failure of self-revelation would be seen as the worst alternative.

Thus if *R* = "God reveals himself" and *B* = "Man believes," then God's ranking of the possibilities would presumably stand as follows:

B & *R*	2
B & -*R*	1
-*B* & *R*	3
-*B* & -*R*	4

God puts a premium on faith. Man's preferences are of course rather different. As *l'homme moyen sceptique*, the alternative -*B* & -*R* may be supposed as his top choice.[95] Man would doubtless welcome the convenience of *undisturbed* disbelief—preferring disbelief as long as God does *not* reveal himself, so that security can be found in the idea that he does not exist. (Disbelief conjoined with overt revelation—being "caught out" in disbelief by a self-revealing God—would clearly be the worst alternative.) On the other hand, if man were to believe, then he would wish for the reassurance of revelation. Thus *B* & *R* is preferable to *B* & -*R*. When human nature is envisaged along the indicated lines, we thus arrive at the following preference schedule for man:

B & R	2
B & $-R$	3
$-B$ & R	4
$-B$ & $-R$	1

Viewing these various preferences in interactive juxtaposition, we arrive at a "game" where man has two choices, to believe or not to believe, and God has two alternatives, to reveal or not to reveal himself. The structure of the resulting game is:

God's choices / *Man's choices*	*R*	*-R*
B	2/2	3/1
-B	4/3	1/4

Neither of the two "players" has a dominant strategy here —a choice that is superior come what may regardless of how the "opponent" chooses. In such cases the decision theoretically "rational"—that is, the *prudent* step—is to select the *maximin* alternative which creates the optimal situation "if worst comes to worst." Since man's maximin option is *B* (and God's is *R*), man would presumably opt for *B* on this basis.

But an omniscient God, realizing that prudent man would follow this line of thought, might well proceed to get his way by opting for *-R*. God would presumably exploit his omniscience to outsmart man. (Nor can man capitalize on this by shifting to *-B*; were he to do so, an omniscient God would realize it.) Thus *B* & *-R* looks to be the reasonable upshot. And so there is no decisive reason why a God who favors the idea of remaining "a hidden God" should not indulge this preference.

A somewhat different, less adversarial line of approach to the issue of revelation is also possible, however. For God will also motivate belief, even in a prudentially minded skeptic, if he is perceived as having a nature that gives some priority to the prospect of rewarding belief by revelation. This revised perspective would lead to viewing God as having the following schedule of putative preferences:

B & *R*	1
B & -*R*	2
-*B* & *R*	3
-*B* & -*R*	4

This preference schedule engenders the following game matrix:

	R	-*R*
B	2/1	3/2
-*B*	4/3	1/4

On contemplating this situation, man would realize that God has a dominant strategy (at *R*). Thus prudence would once more compel man to play safe at *B* to avoid his worst prospect (at -*B* & *R*). To be sure, this preference pattern envisions a God who is prepared to reward belief by self-revelation—the sort of God who responds to the trust of Abraham or who "enters history" and manifests himself to the faithful (or even to doubters like Thomas).

Let us regard the matter from a somewhat different point of view. Consider the "collision-course" situation illustrated by the well-known game of "chicken":

Player B / *Player A*	*Compromise*	*Don't compromise*
Compromise	2/2 (bilateral compromise)	3/1 (*B* prevails over *A*)
Don't compromise	1/3 (*A* prevails over *B*)	4/4 (disaster)

Note that neither player has a dominant strategy—a choice that will serve him better regardless of what the opponent does. However, by forming and declaring an intention *not* to compromise, each player can (try to) compel the other to submit, at the risk of plunging both alike into disaster. (Hence the game's name.) Accordingly, the two players are impelled toward cooperation, despite the fact that each would, in the abstract, undoubtedly prefer noncooperation and "having it all one's own way."[96]

A situation of roughly similar structure could be expected to exist in the context of God's revelation:

Man reaches out to God	*God reaches out to Man*	*Man's preference*	*God's preference*
+	+	2	2
+	–	3-or-4	1
–	+	1	3-or-4
–	–	3-or-4	3-or-4

Here each party inclines positively toward the prospect of a relationship but would prefer the other to take the initiative. In these circumstances the two parties would presumably arrive at the compromise situation of reciprocity (++) in an honest negotiation, settling on what is, from each one's point of view, no better than a second-best alternative. Each is constrained (by prudence alone) to meet the other halfway: neither "has it all his way"—neither secures his first-line preference. It thus becomes understandable how it might be that even a God who would prefer to remain "a hidden God" might be led by the higher exigencies of his own value structure to "come out of his shell"—to reveal himself to Moses and, not content with speaking through the mediation of prophets and messengers, send his own son into the world.

These deliberations illustrate the important difference between *abstract* and *circumstantial* preferences. I would doubtless prefer an exotic luxury automobile in the abstract if "other things were equal." But of course they are not—purchase price, maintenance costs, etc., all come into it. When it comes down to making the critical choice in the prevailing circumstances, I end up "preferring" a more mundane vehicle. And this situation is particularly prominent in those social interaction situations (such as a game or negotiation) in which a conflict of interests must be resolved and some sort of compromise effected. Our abstract preferences may in the final analysis have to be subordinated to circumstantial considerations: in the end we may well wind up "preferring" something different as being optimal "under the circumstances."[97]

*****

The preceding deliberations involve one assumption kept constant throughout—the view of man as prudently self-preoccupied, proceeding with a calculating view to rational self-interest. God's problem may accordingly be seen as that of projecting toward such a creature an image of himself that can motivate belief on ultimately prudential grounds. This is doubtless not the noblest and most elevated sort of religious faith. But some progress has been made all the same. Our analysis has envisioned God as a being who, by appropriately manipulating a developing conception of himself, seeks to *motivate* belief (rather than *constrain* it by coercive *force majeure* intervention), realizing that he is dealing with a relatively selfish prudential creature that ever keeps a weather eye on his own interest. But it emerges that, even within the framework of this rather daunting project, God can still lead man toward a higher, ethically superior conception of his nature.

4. The Relation of Man to God: The Role of (Our Conception of) God's Nature

Consider the structure of a situation of the Pascal's Wager type as set out in Figure 1.

Figure 1

THE STRUCTURE OF CHOICE IN PASCAL'S WAGER SITUATIONS

Result (for Man) as a Function of Reality's Disposition in Affording the Existence of God (E) or Not (-E)

Man's choice between belief (B) and nonbelief (-B)	*E (probability p)*	*-E (probability 1-p)*
B	$+X$	$-x$
$-B$	$-Y$	$+y$

Note: (1) We shall suppose that $+X$ represents a substantial gain, $-Y$ a substantial loss, $-x$ a small loss, and $+y$ a small gain.
(2) p is to be (one's estimate of) the probability that God exists.

On this basis man can compare the expected value of his two choice-alternatives, B and $-B$, as follows:

$$\text{Expected value of } B = (p)(+X) + (1-p)(-x) = p(X+x)-x$$
$$\text{Expected value of } -B = (p)(-Y) + (1-p)(+y) = -p(Y+y)+y$$

It follows that B's expected value is greater than $-B$'s if and only if

$$p\,(X+x)-x > -p\,(Y+y)+y$$
$$p\,(X+Y+x+y) > x+y$$
$$p > \frac{x+y}{(x+y)+(X+Y)} = \frac{1}{1+\dfrac{X+Y}{x+y}}$$

Since $X + Y$ is by hypothesis a large quantity, and $x + y$ a small one, this condition amounts to p's being greater than some *very* small quantity. On this basis belief emerges as man's prudentially best choice if he is prepared to see the probability of God's existence as nontrivial.

However, the rational man can be led to the choice of B over $-B$ regardless of the magnitude of p (as long as p is not 0) in two very different ways.

The first way—the route selected by Pascal himself—is to set X at ∞. For then:

$$\begin{aligned} \text{Expected value of } B &= p(+\infty) + (1-p)(-x) \\ &= +\infty \text{ (as long as } p \text{ is nonzero)} \\ \text{Expected value of } -B &= -p(Y+y) + y \\ &< y \text{ (since } -p(Y+y) \text{ is bound to be negative)} \end{aligned}$$

On this basis the rational man is bound to select B, since its expected value will inevitably exceed that of $-B$ (infinitely!), regardless of how small p may be (as long as p is nonzero). So runs Pascal's argument.

But of course a very differernt route also leads to this same destination. One could set Y at ∞. For then:

$$\begin{aligned} \text{Expected value of } B &= p(X-x) + x \\ &> x \text{ (since } p(X-x) \text{ is bound to be positive)} \\ \text{Expected value of } -B &= p(-\infty) + (1-p)(+y) \\ &= -\infty \text{ (as long as } p \text{ is nonzero)} \end{aligned}$$

And so the rational man, duly guided by expectations, is again bound to select B.

There are thus two very different ways of inducing the rational man to choose B over $-B$: the carrot and the stick. God can make the response to unbelief so unattractive as to scare man off this option, or else make his response to belief so attractive as to lure him thereto. Many assertions to the contrary notwithstanding, it is the latter, specifically positive alternative on which the reasoning of Pascal's Wager actually pivots in its authors's own formulation. It seeks to invite belief through the prospect of reward and not by intimidation through the possibility of eternal hellfire.[98]

The argumentation of Pascal's Wager accordingly rises above the very basest level of motivation that pivots on mere fear. For the argument is so designed as to move us away from

– the jealous, avenging God who constrains belief by threats and intimidation, through fear of punishment and leads us to contemplate

—the kind, generous God who invites belief through the attractiveness of rewards.

The crux here is whether God is seen as generous or as vengeful—whether he is taken to be the sort of God whose priority is to reward belief or one whose priority is to punish disbelief. The question of how man conceives God is thus pivotal—is it to be a God of love or a God of wrath? The actual course of Pascal's argumentation seeks to attract man to belief through the prospect of reward rather than through the threat of punishment. This is already a step in the right direction. (No doubt there is yet a long way to go, seeing that its mode of motivation is still crass and self-interested.) The logic of the argument would work out either way—benefit-seeking and penalty-avoidance both point to the same resolution here. It is theology alone that moves Pascal toward the former choice.

Just how God is conceptualized thus becomes the crucial issue. For example, if God is conceived of as being *so* forgiving as to be virtually indifferent in his treatment of belief and unbelief (so that we shall effectively have that $Y = -X$), then the expected value of $-B$ will exceed that of B, and disbelief becomes the expectation-dominant alternative.[99]

The traditional objection arises that the Wager argument is a many-edged sword. As Diderot complained, "An Imam could reason just as well this way."[100] Argumentation of this sort might lead Pascal's compatriots to the Christian God, but could surely lead Jews to Yahweh, Muslims to Allah, ancient Greeks to the motley crew on Mount Olympus, natives of Momkudo to Mumbo-Jumbo, etc. Is there not an element of "when in Rome, do as the Romans do" to the argument? On such a basis does not the practice of religion come to be degraded to the level of a localized practice like cookery; does it not just become a matter of times and circumstances—of local custom?[101]

This objection can be met by William James's consideration as to what the "live options" are—which possibilities we are prepared to recognize as real and which ones are simply excluded from the range of the practicable.[102] If (like most of us) one is prepared to set the probability of strange gods at zero, the argument cannot point one in their direction.[103] Everything turns on what we are (responsibly) prepared to deem to be *real* possibilities, those having probabilities at any rate greater than zero (no matter how low we may think them to be).

And so the salient point is the centrality of the God-concept that underlies the discussion. With argumentation of the Pascal's Wager type everything is going to turn on just exactly how we envision God. And this, of course, is an issue which the argument itself does not address. It proceeds *ad hominem* under the presupposition that its audience is emplaced within a religious tradition that delineates the sort of God that can be contemplated as a real possibility in traditional Christian terms. And of course if this is indeed our stance, then the fact that others take a different view of the matter is simply beside the point for us.

*****

It is clear that Pascal's position is predicated on a Judeo-Christian monotheistic view of God. But why only this one possibility?—as George Santayana liked to ask on behalf of other gods. Suppose, for example, that one thought it to be a real possibility for one of two (mutually exclusive) conceivable gods to turn out to be real: the Christian's God (G) who, should he exist, rewards belief and forgives disbelief, and an alternative all-powerful jealous god (G') who, should *he* exist, would direly punish disbelievers—Christians above all. We would then arrive at a more complex situation:

	Result (for Man) as a Function of Reality's Disposition		
Man's choice	*G exists* (probability p)	*G′ exists* (probability p')	*No god exists* (probability $1-p-p'$)
Believe in G	$+\infty$	$-\infty$	0
Believe in G'	$-x$	$+y$	0
No belief	$-z$	$-\infty$	0

Here a policy of disaster-avoidance would automatically underwrite belief in G'—unless of course $p' = 0$.

Suppose, on the other hand, that G' (like G) were tolerant of disbelief (with those $-\infty$'s changed to finite negative quantities). Belief in G would then once more become the prudentially indicated choice.

Indeed it might be argued even if one believes that there might be any one of several possible jealous gods, say n of them, a Pascal-type argument would still tell against atheism as such. To see this, consider the situation of Table 1 (based, for simplicity, on the supposition that $n = 3$):

Table 1

THE PROSPECT OF A PLURALITY OF JEALOUS GODS

	Results for Man if			
Believe in	G_1 *exists*	G_2 *exists*	G_3 *exists*	*None exists*
G_1	$+X$	$-V$	$-V$	$-x$
G_2	$-V$	$+X$	$-V$	$-x$
G_3	$-V$	$-V$	$+X$	$-x$
None	$-V$	$-V$	$-V$	$+y$

Assumptions: X is large, V is large, x and y are relatively small.

The atheistic choice of believing in none of the G_i is the worst option. In this case there is no bonus for being right; if none of the G_i exist, we are safe in any event. Otherwise it is only by choosing some G_i or other (perhaps even at random) that we have any chance of averting disaster.[104]

Theism is now not a matter of hoping for benefit but of "clutching at straws" to avert catastrophe.[105]

Again, if we are prepared to contemplate several alternative gods, each, as it were, bidding for our belief, then matters will take on the rather different look of Table 2.

Table 2

THE PROSPECT OF A PLURALITY OF GENEROUS GODS

	Result (for Man) as a Function of Reality's Disposition		
Man's choice	*G_1 exists* (probability p_1)	*G_2 exists* (probability p_2)	*No god exists* (probability $1-p_1-p_2$)
Believe in G_1	$+\infty$	$-u$	0
Believe in G_2	$-v$	$+\infty$	0
No belief	$-x$	$-y$	0

The first two alternatives will *both* have infinite positive expectations (as long as the probabilities at issue are nonzero). If we are to sell ourselves to the highest celestial bidder, as it were, there seems no better course than to do so in line with the greater probability, according as $p_1 \lesseqgtr p_2$.[106]

*****

Pascal's Wager is predicated on having a view of God's nature. (How, after all, could someone deliberate on the matter who did not take a position here?) In the background of the reasoning there lies a presupposition of the form: "If there is a god-like being at all, then it is going to be one of such-and-such a sort." The person who does not endorse such a thesis regarding the nature of God—who rejects claims to the effect that God is bound to have a certain suitable *modus operandi*—is not going to be reached by the sort of argument Pascal developed.

Throughout these sorts of decision-making situations it makes a crucial difference how one views the opponent's value posture. Suppose for example that the choice situation I confront is as follows, and is known by my opponent to be such:

Opponent's choices / *My choices*	(i)	(ii)
(i)	2/?	3/?
(ii)	1/?	4/?

Being utterly in the dark as to how the opponent evaluates outcomes, I would presumably opt for my alternative (i), which prevents a worst-possible outcome. But of course if I have definite beliefs about how the opponent evaluates the outcomes, I might well see this situation in the following light:

Opponent's choices / *My choices*	(i)	(ii)
(i)	2/1	3/3
(ii)	1/2	4/4

Realizing that my opponent must select his alternative (i) because of its seriatim dominance, I can safely opt for my alternative (ii) to realize an optimal result. One's view of the opponent's outcome-valuations will, obviously, have a crucial effect on the rational choice of a course of action in such interactive situations. Rational deliberation about God's existence in the practical mode will hinge crucially on how we conceive his nature.

These deliberations point to an important conclusion. A Pascal-type argument does not lead inexorably to a Pascal-type conclusion. Everything is going to turn on just exactly what sort of a god we are prepared to contemplate. The reasoning of the Wager is conditional: those who espouse a certain concept of God ought (prudentially) to believe in him.

Of course, one need not be cock-sure about the matter. One can be like the Uncle Toby of Laurence Sterne's *Tristram Shandy,* who "never spoke of the being and natural attributes of God, but with diffidence and hesitation" (bk. 8, ch. 19). But against the total skeptic, who holds that we can know nothing of God, Pascal's argument can carry no weight at all. (Then, too, the argument would be of little avail if one contemplates a God who rewards only people who reach him by a route devoid of considerations of self-interest.[107])

Critics of Pascal's Wager object:

> In thus limiting our betting choice to two, Pascal makes a gigantic, unwarranted, and false assumption . . . that there is only one Hell threatening possibility, to be matched against the annihilation-threatening no-God possibility.[108]

Or again:

> The argument . . . assumes that there is only one possible version of theism, when in fact there are many possible gods in whom one might believe. . . . [T]he gambling theist may find that he has backed the wrong horse. . . . Let us suppose, conservatively, that there are 100 possible jealous gods from which he has to choose. Suddenly the force of the argument is deflected: there is no percentage in favor of belief at all, since there is an overwhelming likelihood of being punished in any case.[109]

The point is quite right but totally irrelevant. It is right because the person who is realistically worried about all those myriad possible jealous gods is indeed going to find Pascal's Wager unconvincing. But the fact remains the argument is simply not addressed to this person (if such there be). It is addressed to those nominal Christians, whose name is legion, who do indeed espouse the god-conception on which the argument is premised. For most people the idea of God has its limits—the range of god-possibilities they are prepared to consider as *real* possibilities (prospects whose probability is nonzero) is one at most.[110]

The Wager argument as it stands presupposes a background of slack Christian religiosity. As Antony Flew rightly notes, Pascal's argument will not underwrite his conclusion for someone who envisions a god who will consign Christians to eternal hell and non-Christians to eternal heaven.[111] But why anyone should think this consideration to constitute an *objection* to the argument is puzzling. No argument can be expected to do more than persuade those who accept its premises (which in Pascal's case, of course, relate to the *nature* of God, not his *existence*).

Again and again over the years critics have complained:

> (Pascal) seems to have made the entirely unrealistic assumption that by choosing a way of life one is faced with two options alone when, of course, there are indefinitely many. First of all it may be noted that a belief in God itself splits up into many distinct beliefs, namely a belief in God as conceived and prescribed by the various monotheistic religions. Each of these religions promise eternal reward to those who pursue them and Pascal provides no argument to help one in selecting the right belief among these. Or consider . . . a very powerful demon who rules this universe and who rewards all those and only those who deny the existence of an omnipotent and omnibenevolent God, by granting them eternal bliss in the world to come.[112]

But this sort of objection also overlooks the nature and purpose of Pascal's argumentation. It is emphatically *not* concerned with the religionless outsider who wants to shop for a religion and proposes to see which side has the best bargain on offer—the person who has no views about God and wants to know which way to go. It is addressed only to people who have a very definite sort of view of what God (should he exist) would be like—to the person who is committed to the Christian *idea* of God but hesitates about believing in him.

The salient point is that while Wager-style argumentation

can in principle be developed in the context of very different god-conceptions (Christian, Jewish, Muslim, Hindu, polytheist, etc.), it cannot be developed *in vacuo.* One contemporary critic of Pascal objected that:

> This reasoning suits all religions; that which proves too much proves nothing. It only proves the necessity of having some religion, but not the Christian religion.[113]

This criticism is altogether misguided. One cannot successfully employ a Pascal-type course of reasoning to argue for the existence of a god-in-general—regardless of any and every sort of conception of him—and then raise (independently) the question of whether whatever god may exist has the character of the Christian God. Such a recasting would not enable the argument to get off the ground, owing to the unavailability of the critically necessary data. The argument is so structured that only if we have a suitably definite god-concept to provide for the needed premises can we arrive at its theological conclusion.

Pascal, as we have seen, insists on beginning with the question-shift from "Does God exist?" to "Is it *prudent to believe* that God exists?" The answer to *this* question will obviously hinge on our views regarding (1) the nature of prudence and (2) the nature of God. The former (we shall suppose) is not problematic: what is to be at issue is the sort of prudential rationality explicated by decision-theory. As regards the second item (the nature of God) this is of course not a matter for private decision. We are no more at liberty to adopt a God-concept at variance with that of our circumambient tradition than we are to adopt one of a terrier or an elm tree. I am no freer to provide a purely idiosyncratic answer to "What is the nature of God?" than I am to provide a purely idiosyncratic answer to "What is the nature of the sun (i.e., is it a divine being, a great fire, a large-scale nuclear reactor, etc.)?" In the absence of new fundamental discoveries the best we can do here is to adopt—in essentials, at any rate—the answer that is standard in our culture-context. Thus, naturally enough, Pascal subscribed to the idea that the appropriate answer to the question of God's nature is that provided by the Christian theological tradition. And this is surely plausible. For *our* purposes the question of other peoples' gods is clearly as irrelevant as the question of other peoples' suns. What matters is how *we* ourselves conceive of God.

Pascal's approach takes essentially the following line:

> Let us not talk about God in the strictly *ontological* mode, and ask "Is there a God?" And let us not proceed in the epistemological mode and ask the evidential/probative question, "What evidence have we for claiming that God exists?" Rather, let us proceed in a conjointly conceptual and pragmatic order, contemplating the *concept* of God (rather than God *per se*) and asking the normative/pragmatic question "Is this concept such that its object *deserves* credence?"

The deliberations at work in Pascal's Wager can be thought of as a matter of coming to terms with a concept. (In *this* respect it is like Anselm's ontological argument.) What is at issue is an interaction (a game or negotiation, as it were) with an *idea* of ours—namely a God-conception. The question is to determine whether or not this idea deserves credence—whether or not it is sensible to believe in this God whose nature it depicts. The causal source or origin of this idea is for the moment irrelevant. Did we simply make it up (as atheists always insist), did we find it innately implanted in our mind (as Descartes has it), does it brood like a spirit over the waters of our historical situation (as with Hegel)? It just doesn't matter! What matters is that it is there and that we have got to come to terms with it. The salient thing, from Pascal's point of view, is that when we ask if the idea *deserves* credence we should construe "deserve" in the broadest sense—one that embraces not simply evidential considerations alone but prudential considerations as well.

5. The Dialectic of Heart and Mind: A Contest between Two Sides of Man's Nature

A dualistic conception of human nature lies in the background of the Wager argument. Pascal sees our human nature as having two sides; let us call them "heart" and "mind" respectively:

	Intellectual (cognitive) attributes	*Motivational (affective) attributes*
"Heart"	emotional, fideistic, trusting, theistically receptive	generosity, trust, concern for others
"Mind"	coldly rational, calculating, judgmental, theistically skeptical	self-interest, self-centeredness, "What's in it for me?"

Mind's tool is discursive reason and evidential cognition; heart proceeds by way of intuition and affective inclination. The natural habitat of Mind is mathematics (its ethos is an *espirit de géométrie*); the natural habitat of Heart is spontaneous sentiment and intuitive appraisal (its ethos is an *espirit de finesse*).

These two sides of our nature are in significant measure independent, and neither prevails automatically in matters of thought or action. Neither Mind nor Heart can force the other's hand; neither can simply dominate the other and have it all its own way. Specifically, each can come down either way in the matter of God's existence. Accordingly, four situations can in theory obtain:

	Mind	*Heart*
(1)	*B*	*B*
(2)	*B*	*-B*
(3)	*-B*	*B*
(4)	*-B*	*-B*

Each party is free to evaluate and rank these four alternative situations as it wishes. There is, however, some premium on coherence in matters of thought, belief, and action—on self-consistency and inner agreement. For a lack of concurrence means that both sides lose out, since dissonance is in some degree stressful and unpleasant for both parties—and particularly so for good old rational Mind. The negativity of such discord is something that we must (and that Mind certainly does) recognize.

The overall ranking that results will accordingly be as follows:

Mind	*Heart*	*M-ranking*	*H-ranking*
B	*B*	2	1
B	*-B*	4	4
-B	*B*	3	2
-B	*-B*	1	3

Mind ranks $-B_m$ & $-B_h$ first because of its inclination to disbelief and its rationality-conditioned preference for agreement. Its low tolerance for cognitive discord leads it (reluctantly) to put B_m & B_h into second place, relegating the two discordant alternatives to the bottom of its rankings. Heart has a very different set of preferences. It wants to opt for *B* regardless of consistency. (It inclines to see harmony as a fetish of Mind, which it regards as making a mere desideratum into something absolute.)

Placing these rankings in interactive juxtaposition, a game situation of the following description is seen to result:

Mind \ *Heart*	*B*	*-B*
B	2/1	4/4
-B	3/2	1/3

Heart has a dominant choice here, namely *B*, which yields a preferred outcome no matter which way Mind chooses.

Mind, recognizing this (clever fellow!), will secure its best option at *B*. The upshot is that mind's commitment to consistency has overridden its abstract, "Other things equal" preference for *-B* over *B*. Wholly without guile, Heart manages to force Mind's hand by creating a situation where other things are not equal.

This result illustrates a phenomenon not infrequent in human affairs—the victory of emotion over reason. Its very *reasonableness* leads reason to defeat through its inclination "to see both sides of the question" and its capacity "to make the best of a bad situation." Mind's basic dedication to consistency and coherence enables Heart to induce it to yield.

The deeper purpose of Pascal's Wager argument emerges from such an analysis of the dialectic of Mind and Heart. For its mission is to reconcile a reluctant Mind to going along with belief through an appeal made in its own terms —the lure of self-interest.

To be sure, if Mind were dead set on disbelief, the M-rankings of the preceding analysis would be altered. The "game" would take the form:

Heart / *Mind*	*B*	*-B*
B	3/1	4/4
-B	2/2	1/3

Each party now has a dominant strategy: prudence and inclination alike would drive Heart to *B* and Mind to *-B*. The basis of compromise on a mutually acceptable result would be removed: the two parties would simply "agree to disagree." Cognitive dissonance would now ensue. As matters actually stand, however, the Wager argument endeavors to induce Mind—on the basis of its own self-interestedly prudential terms—to reach a compromise where Heart's demands receive due recognition.

Pascal's talk of Heart and Mind is designed to recognize

that there are different sides to our nature. Mind is not the be-all and end-all of cognition: reason is insufficient to settle the great issues of and by itself. Pascal holds, contrary to Descartes, that the first principles of knowledge and obligation are *not* rationally demonstrable: "principles are felt, propositions proved, and both with certainty, although by different means."[114] The impetus to faith in God comes from Heart, not Mind: *Dieu sensible au coeur, non à la raison.* And heart does not *convince* reason but merely *induces* it to go along by way of compromise. Our thought-world is ruled by a parliament, as it were, where different interests are all represented. This provides the setting of an internal negotiation toward a resolution where all these various interests of different "estates" are duly accommodated—each recognizing the other's requirements in some degree. Pascal's approach calls for something no theoretician has yet worked out—a parliamentary model of the human intellect where what is finally decided upon in rational deliberation is not the product of the unilaterally decreed requirements of a single faculty or interest, but a reasonable compromise between the potentially divergent pull of diverse elements.[115]

6. The Rationality of Trust and Hope

Pascal's Wager argument is, in effect, a plea for trust—for trust in the great promises of the Christian religion. As such it is structurally akin to a whole family of other arguments in favor of trust in potentially problematic resources.

Why should one have trust in the "state of the art" in matters of medicine, say, or macroeconomics? Their present performance gives no basis for unalloyed confidence, and this consideration becomes all the more telling where the "present" at issue is taken to be that of several generations ago. We must have every expectation that the present will be equally deficient from the vantage point of the future. The historical record of these disciplines is a mosaic of mistakes. Why should one trust expert "guidance" in areas where one realizes full well how weak a reed the experts we lean on actually are.

A very common form of practical decision-situation has the following structure:

	Trust justified	*Trust not justified*
Take a chance and trust	1	2
Don't trust: play safe	3	2

The repeated 2s indicate a tie for second place. The alternatives are essentially indifferent. The situation is viewed in the light that if trust is *not* justified, then we sustain effectively equal losses either way. In *that* case it just doesn't matter—we're in the soup to roughly the same degree, do what we will. On the other hand, if we "play safe" and fail to exercise trust when doing so is in fact justified, then worst has come to worst—we'd wind up kicking ourselves, and regret is superadded to loss. In these circumstances the alternative of trust is in a position of (weak) dominance: we cannot fare significantly worse by adopting it, and we might possibly do better. There is indeed an alternative to trust, but the option it provides is unappealing.

There are many instances of this generic type. One arises in the context of interpersonal relations, when we have got to trust and risk disappointment to make things work out. ("Faint heart ne'er won fair lady.") The human situation is such that in many sorts of cases we face the operative principle "We may as well make the effort—there's nothing much to be lost by trying." An analysis of this sort can be applied in various belief-in cases (belief in ourself, in other people, in "the system," in God), as long as the situation is such that in the unhappy event that belief is *not* justified, the result is very much equally unfortunate. In all such cases we may as well trust because all is lost if we don't. William James insightfully stressed that this line of thought validates trust in many collaborative ventures:

> A social organism of any sort whatever, large or small, is what it is because each member proceeds to his own duty with a trust that the other members will simultaneously do theirs. Wherever a desired result is achieved by the co-operation of many independent persons, its existence as a fact is pure consequence of the precursive faith in one another of those immediately concerned. A government, an army, a commercial system, a ship, a college, an athletic team, all exist on this condition, without which not only is nothing achieved, but nothing is even attempted. There are, then, cases where a fact cannot come to be at all unless a preliminary faith exists in the coming.[116]

This general line of thought also lies at the root of Pascal's Wager argument. It urges us to gamble on trust—in its case in God—on the basis of the idea that in so doing nothing much is to be lost and everything to be gained.

*****

A particularly interesting situation arises in the case of personal interactions. Let T = "I trust him" and t = "He trusts me." Four situations can obtain, which, if I am a prudently suspicious individual, would rank as follows:

T	t	2
T	$-t$	4
$-T$	t	1
$-T$	$-t$	3

That is, I want him to trust me, yet cautiously distrust him myself, and see as the worst case that where my own trust goes unreciprocated.

Now if he takes the same attitude toward me, we shall have:

	T	$-T$
T	2/2	4/1
$-T$	1/4	3/3

If this is how the situation stands, then, clearly, $-T$ dominates from my point of view. (If I opt for $-T$, then I fare better than otherwise no matter how he chooses to proceed.) And, of course, the situation looks exactly the same from his point of view. On this basis we arrive straightaway at the 3/3 resolution—despite the fact that the mutually preferred 2/2 result is available to us.

The preceding situation is in fact that of the much-discussed Prisoner's Dilemma.[117] Many treatments of game theory and decision theory regard this situation as a paradox which shows that the "rational" thing to do can nevertheless be *suboptimal.*

But this is a profoundly erroneous conclusion. It would only obtain if one were to follow the common approach of economists and decision theorists in construing rationality as purely and solely a matter of prudential safety first. Only by taking the (surely mistaken) step of insisting that "rationality" is utterly risk aversive—in that it requires an uncompromising commitment to prudential safety first—can we say that it is *rationality* that is at odds with *optimality* in the game situation at issue.

If, on the contrary, we construe rationality as the *intelligent* pursuit of one's ends—in a way that gives weight but not necessarily predominance to considerations of safety and risk—then clearly the situation in view is no longer one where rationality conflicts with optimality at all. But then, of course, a choice of $-T$ is no longer the automatically "rational" course.

Most economists and decision theorists see trust as inherently at odds with prudential rationality and are thus baffled by the "paradoxical" situation of the Prisoner's Dilemma which indicates that prudence-ignoring trust may in fact conduce to self-interest. But this, of course, is absurd. Trust (as the example clearly shows) may well prove advantageous. A rationality of intelligent self-interest conflicts not with *trust* in this case, but only with safety-first *prudence.*

The lesson is straightforward. Nothing in the nature of

things has decreed that there is something inherently irrational about trust and its congeners: hope and faith.

*****

This orientation toward trust and hope helps to highlight the crucial aspect of futurity in Pascal's as in any other wager situation—the matter of "how things will turn out." Christian faith, after all, is in significant degree a stance toward the future—a matter of an eschatological hope-and-expectation that there will come a time when the scales are lifted from our eyes, the veil of unseeing torn away, and our entry into another realm realized. In a "waiting game" of this sort, as in any game, this sort of attitude to the future cannot be based on *knowledge.* If I already knew the outcome (knew, say, that my team could win because the game is "fixed"), then there is little point in the exercise, and what is at issue is not really a game or gamble at all. A belief in the religious mode of hope-and-expectation is to be something very different (in character, though not necessarily in content) from a belief in the epistemic mode of evidence and inference.

7. "Pascal's Wager"-Style Argumentation in Ethics and Epistemology

Pascal's Wager argument constitutes an endeavor to motivate religiosity through its being advantageous for the realization of our interests. As such it has been greeted on virtually all sides with howls of condemnation and derision—reproached time and again as representing a crass and unworthy appeal to selfish advantage.

Throughout this aversive reaction, however, it is conveniently forgotten that there is an ancient and widely respected tradition for arguing in exactly this sort of way on behalf of morality: the Epicurean tactic of supporting morality on the basis of advantage.[118] This tradition was revived in Pascal's own day by his younger contemporary

Thomas Hobbes, who argued for social cooperation under the aegis of moral rules on the ground that this averts a mode of life that would otherwise be "nasty, brutish, and short." To be sure, this position has not met with universal approval—what philosophical position has?! But it has always received a respectful hearing and has been defended from Hobbes's day to ours by a succession of able social, political, and legal theorists. In this regard its fate stands in stark contrast to the reception of Pascal's Wager among philosophers and theologians.

Figure 2

A Neo-Epicurean Legitimation of Morality

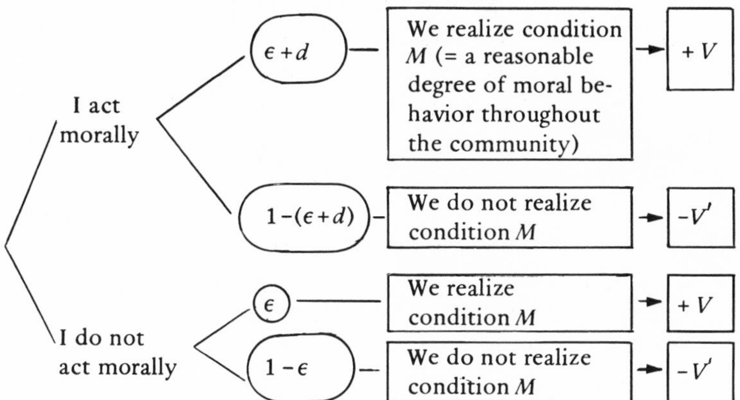

Note: Here d is, in effect, the differential increment that my acting morally makes to the probability (ϵ) of the moral project's realization.

And yet the Epicurus-Hobbes line is a close cousin of Pascal's argument. It supports morality on exactly the same basis on which Pascal supports religiosity—personal advantage. To see this we should note that the choice situation at issue is depicted as per Figure 2. Here we have it that:

$$\text{EV (top alternative)} = (\epsilon + d)\,(V) + (1 - \epsilon - d)\,(-V')$$

$$\text{EV (bottom alternative)} = \epsilon\,(V) + (1 - \epsilon)\,(-V')$$

Observe that

$$\text{EV (top)} > \text{EV (bottom)} \text{ iff } d(V+V') > 0 \text{ iff } d > 0$$

As long as *d* is not 0, that is, as long as my acting morally makes some positive difference (however small) to the chance of the moral project's being realized (perhaps by encouraging others), the top alternative will routinely prevail. Or, put differently, it will do so as long as my failing to act morally might (should I be caught out and thus discourage others) detract therefrom in some small way. And, after all, there is always *some* prospect of this. (We can safely rule out Plato's supposition of the Ring of Gyges.)

To be sure, the preceding argument is problematic as it stands. It overlooks the fact that I might pay a price for acting morally. To render this omission irrelevant it would be sufficient to adopt the (relatively plausible) supposition that the relative utility of the moral order (V) and the disutility of its failure $(-V')$ is so hugely discrepant as to be effectively infinite. In this event we would obtain a close cousin to the reasoning of Pascal's Wager argument.

With Hobbes and Pascal alike we have a course of legitimation that pivots on a potential advantage. But if a *morality* based on interest is not thereby rendered altogether unworthy, why (the prejudice of *odium theologicum* apart) should a *religiosity* that is so based automatically be so? Why should sauce for the moral goose not be sauce for the theological gander as well? After all, in neither case are we asking the argument to bear the entire burden—to support the whole of morality or the whole of religiosity on its back. There is no reason to think it could not usefully carry part of the load.

*****

Again, consider the case of man's cognitive condition. The issue of the *correctness* of our currently purported scientific "knowledge" of the world is far from unproblematic. Scientific progress is scientific change; seldom is the science of an era endorsed lock, stock, and barrel by its successors a hundred years or so further on. Indeed, even our intellect's ability to afford us effective guidance amidst the shoals and narrows of a difficult world is something regarding which we have no iron-clad guarantee. Rational action in this world is inevitably predicated on an evidence-transcending trust that all will go well. We cannot even be certain that the world will continue, from one moment to the next, to be a safe home for creatures constituted as we are. Our ability to live and learn in this world hinges on the enduring validity of many facts regarding our bodies, our minds, and our environment. To judge or act rationally is to have trust in the efficacy of our intellectual and physical operations within nature.[119]

To be sure, one cannot provide a knock-down refutation of skepticism in the theoretical-evidential order of reason. All we can do is to show that the price of holding a skeptical position is too high. The argument we can develop against radical *cognitive* skepticism is an argument in the *practical* order of reason—an argument of roughly the same sort as that developed by Pascal against atheism/agnosticism, i.e., against religious skepticism.

Even the most radical of ancient skeptics endorsed trust in the appearances of everyday experience (the *phenomena*) to guide us aright in life's practical affairs (though they certainly do not provide for knowledge, *epistēmē*). As they saw it, we are rationally entitled to act on the indications of the phenomena in the confident expectation that matters will turn out well. There is little choice about this matter. We have no real alternative but to trust in the cognitively cooperative disposition of the natural order of things. We cannot preestablish the appropriateness of this trust by somehow showing, in advance of events, that it is actually warranted. Rather, its rationale is that without it we remove the basis on which alone creatures such as ourselves can confidently live a life of effective thought and action. As pragmatists of many sorts have always argued, cognition too is in no position to disdain a pragmatic legitimation with reference to interest. This practicalistic defense of human cognition was initially deployed by the ancient skeptics. It was revived in Renaissance skepticism, reiterated by David Hume, reformulated in an evolutionary vein by various late nineteenth-century thinkers, and refurbished on a grand scale by William James. There is a longstanding and eminently respectable tradition of using in defense of human cognition the same sort of pragmatic rationale that is at issue in Pascal's Wager.

*****

As these considerations indicate, pragmatic validation has been deployed in three major contexts in the history of philosophy.

(1) With respect to the *moral* project. The aim here is the rational validation of morality. Why should men be moral? (After all, this may not pay off—indeed, we may lose out by it.) The response at issue runs: "Only if they themselves put their shoulder to the wheel and do their part can men further the realization of a better order of things in human affairs." The position envisions a validation of morality not in intrinsic terms (virtue is its own reward) but in goal-oriented ones (virtue is the pathway to a better order of things for men-in-general). This line of thought was espoused in antiquity by the Epicureans.

(2) With respect to the *cognitive* project. The main task here is the validation of sense-perception against the Pyrrhonian skeptic. "If I'm going to attain knowledge about the world at all, then I've got to trust the sense in at least some sorts of circumstance." This line of thought was devised by the mitigated skeptics of the Middle Academy and developed by various modern pragmatists.

(3) With respect to the *religious* project. Validation of religious faith and observance. "If there is to be any

chance at all for me to realize the great good that religion promises, I have got to take that initial step of enrolling myself within the community of believers." This is the thrust of Pascal's argument.

Reasoning of an essentially parallel structure is at issue in all three cases.

Rationality can be viewed as including two (closely interrelated) components, rationality in belief and rationality in action—cognitive and pragmatic rationality. However, any temptation to see a sharp dichotomy here was decisively undermined in the mitigated skepticism of the Middle Academy, which opened up an essentially practice-oriented epistemological justification of accepting and acting on our everyday sense-based view of the world. This line of thought was prefigured by the Epicureans, who applied it to the validation of morality, maintaining that moral action conduces optimally to the successful conduct of the affairs of life. Pascal analogously provides a practical validation of accepting (and acting on) the teachings of our religious heritage. All three of these demarches deploy the same basic idea. The Epicureans saw considerations of effective action as governing our morality (our other-involving actions). The mitigated skeptics saw them as governing our cognition (our factual knowledge). Pascal saw them as governing our religion (our religious beliefs and practices). A fundamental analogy of process obtains throughout these three courses of pragmatic validation.[120]

8. The Centrality of Hope

The skeptics have always insisted—and rightly so—that we cannot *prove* in advance that we will not go wrong by trusting the senses. But, of course, what we can do is to establish that if we reject the senses, we cut ourselves off from any prospect of factual knowledge. Again, for moral agency to be effective (i.e., to conduce, on the whole, to "the general good") we require a similar degree of trust. If we reject morality and fail to do our bit toward the realization of the moral project, we impede the prospects of its realization. The religious case is similar. We cannot prove that the religious life will enable us to realize our desired ends; all we can do is to recognize that without religion we diminish the prospects of their realization. And much the same story also holds with regard to trust in oneself and one's capabilities, in other people, in the cooperativeness of nature, etc.

There are no guarantees that our ventures in trust, trying, belief, and the like are going to prove successful. That our trust is actually warranted in such circumstances (trust in ourselves, in our cognitive facilities, in other people, etc.) is something we cannot in the nature of things ascertain in advance of events. A conjunction of trust with hope and faith is germane alike to the cognitive project, the moral project, the religious project. Throughout, we have to conduct our operations under conditions of risk, without assured confidence of outcome and without advance guarantees of success. We deal in all these contexts with courses of action whose efficacy is a matter of hope and whose rationalization is a matter of this-or-nothing-better argumentation. Pascal's argument moves within the orbit of this line of thought.[121]

In trusting the senses, in being moral, in being religious, we always take a gamble. Whenever we place our faith somewhere, we run the risk of being let down and disappointed in the end. Nevertheless, it seems perfectly reasonable to bet on the general trustworthiness of the senses, the general reliability of our fellowmen, and the general validity of our religious tradition. For while no guarantees can be issued, one may as well venture, since if venturing fails, the cause is lost anyhow—we have no more promising alternatives to turn to. We cannot preestablish success; we can do no more than realize a precondition of its possibility. ("Nothing ventured, nothing gained.") It is a matter of "this or nothing better": trusting, trying, making the effort is a policy by which we might well gain with nothing much to lose. Pascal's resort to sophisticated practical reasoning is underpinned by the shrewd psychological insight that despair brings no benefits and hope exacts few penalties.

What is at issue throughout is the centrality of *hope*: we hope that our moral struggle will prove availing. Similarly, to join the community of religious believers is a matter of enrolling in a confraternity of hope.[122] Its pivot is a faith in God—a godliness which alone "enables us to be crowned with the hope of the ultimate achievement of all our good ends," as Kant puts it.[123] For Pascal religious faith accordingly roots not in cognitive certainty but in hope. His object in elaborating the Wager argument and its ramifications was to reorient matters from a theology of mind to a theology of heart—from a theology of proof and demonstration to a theology of trust and hope in the ultimate meaningfulness of human endeavor.

Hope can have small beginnings; it can begin in the feebleness of "wish for" and slowly move toward the greater strength of expectation. To hope for things one cannot expect to attain and to aspire to things one scarcely dare hope for is what makes someone truly a human being. The person who lives by reason alone is in a way splendid—but in a way that is effectively inhuman. We might stand in awe of him but would hesitate to want him as a friend. Important though it is, the place of reason in life's affairs is not all-inclusive. To aspire beyond the realm of cold rationality is in its way something admirable and good.

To be sure, hope is appropriate only as long as the door of possibility is open—it makes little sense to hanker after what cannot possibly be had. And this is where Pascal's recourse to skepticism comes into play. It removes knowledge to make way for hope. As long as no decisive, knockdown considerations enter in to foreclose the matter, "hope springs eternal in the human breast."

As Pascal sees it, faith is justified because it is the assurance of things hoped for. A world without hope is a bleak and forbidding place—a literally inhuman emptiness devoid of any prospect for meaningful life. The extinction of hope is the ultimate evil.

IV
Is a Practically Grounded Faith Unworthy?

1. Is an Appeal to Interest Unworthy?

In 1899 G. E. Moore read a paper on "Religious Belief" to the Sunday Essay Society in Cambridge which, after scornfully dismissing religious belief, went on to remark that "[As regards Pascal's contention that] in our state of doubt we should decide for that belief which promises the greater reward, I have nothing to say of it except that it seems to me absolutely wicked."[124] This reaction is commonplace. Almost unanimously, commentators denounce the element of crassness that is present in Pascal's Wager argument and see it as blasphemous to support religious belief by considerations of prudence.

The French philosopher Jules Lachelier tried to support Pascal by the defensive move of maintaining that the usual construction of the Wager is incorrect in that it inappropriately leaves out of account Pascal's recognition of the inherent benefits of the religious life (viz., the realization of a lifestyle worthy of human dignity) and the negativities endemic to a self-centered, pleasure-seeking, worldly life (viz., the frustrations inherent in the insatiability of human appetites).[125] Lachelier's defensive reformulation of Pascal's argument is sketched in Figure 1. It envisages a straightforward dominance situation where one *gains* by opting for faith no matter how things eventuate. If God exists, belief yields great otherworldly rewards; if he does not, it yields substantial this-worldly ones via the rewards intrinsic to religious life. The alternative of belief affords superior benefits either way.

Figure 1

PASCAL'S WAGER ACCORDING TO LACHELIER

	Reality's alternatives	
Man's alternatives	God exists	God does not exist
Have faith and seek to improve oneself	Gain a life worthy of human dignity AND a blissful afterlife in heaven	Gain a life worthy of human dignity
Be an atheist and lead a completely selfish life	Lose a life worthy of human dignity AND a blissful afterlife in heaven	Lose a life worthy of human dignity

This interesting argument, however, just is not Pascal's. And for very good reason. For if this were indeed Pascal's argumentation, then—for one thing—the entire issue would simply be one of a straightforward victory by dominance, without any recourse to probabilistic considerations. And this would unravel the whole fabric of Pascal's reasoning in the Wager argument. The positivity of "a life worthy of human dignity" would preponderate over the matter of costs, and the need for Pascal's probabilistic, decision-theoretic turn would be averted. The whole probabilistic turn of Pascal's reasoning would become a needless complication. The factor of cost or price which crucially enters into Pascal's reasoning in a way that outruns the resources of dominance argumentation would now be entirely otiose. There would be no need to carry Pascal's argument beyond what in actuality is simply its first, introductory stage. Pascal is thus defended as a theologian at the clearly problematic cost of making him an incompetent reasoner.

Then, too, if the argument were as Lachelier depicts it, the choice at issue would be decided entirely on the basis of this-worldly considerations. (The burden of argumentation now pivots on how matters stand in this world: what comes after those ANDs now becomes wholly irrelevant to the choice, as long as it is the same thing in both cases.) But the matter of *this-worldly* achievement—be it of something noble (like human dignity) or of something crass (like personal advantage)—is clearly not the *point d'appui* of the Wager argument. Pascal is concerned specifically to compare worldly with other-worldly advantages and to *weigh* their respective claims. He wants explicitly to invite us to contrast the hollow benefits of this world with the deeper satisfactions of an ideal order. Pascal's argumentation is crucially concerned with the next world, not with this one. Lachelier's well-intentioned reconstruction not only distorts and emasculates Pascal's reasoning but makes him out as a relatively shallow theologian as well.

To be sure, Lachelier's move in the direction of the argumentation that maintains that one would be better off in *this* life by becoming a believer is by no means unpopular. People often argue roughly as follows:

> Interest bears on the justification of belief in God because there is a deep *need* on man's part for God to exist. Without this belief human life would be empty and meaningless.

This attractive view—found in William James[126] and various lesser lights—also recommends belief in God on the basis of its potential advantages for one's life in *this* world. But it differs crucially from Pascal's own approach in its contemplation of the *earthly* rewards of lessened anxiety, greater social acceptance, etc.—in sum, in its *Paris vaut bien la messe* approach to religion. This sort of thing is not going on in Pascal. He does not argue, as other prudentially minded theologians have, on the principle: "If you live according to religious precepts and principles, then you will find the living of *this* life substantially more satisfying than you otherwise would." Homilists often dwell upon the joys of the religious life and the emptiness of fruitless self-sufficiency here on earth. But this is not Pascal's line. For better or for worse he is not a precursor of the Dale Carnegie school of theology. Throughout the Wager argument his eyes are firmly fixed on the next world, not on this one.

*****

On first sight the reasoning of the Wager argument may perhaps seem akin to buttering up our rich widowed aunt on the chance of being remembered in her will. But this involves a grave misreading of the situation. For one thing, Pascal's argumentation is an appeal to prudence all right—but prudence transformed. Ordinary prudence turns on the distinction between immediate gratification and long-term self-interest. But, as Pascal sees it, Christianity revolutionizes "the long term" at issue through its postulation of *the life to come* in the next world. This otherworldly orientation clearly transforms the nature of prudence and renders it less crass than it otherwise would be. Pascal's argumentation represents an appeal which at any rate transcends the level of nest-feathering hither-worldliness: its attention is focused not upon *this* world but upon the world to come. Pascal's argument too is an argument from advantage, but the possibilities it contemplates are at any rate those removed from the immediacy of *worldly* advantage.

The very crassness of its orientation to self-interest and self-advantage enables the Wager argument to raise some tough questions. It extends an invitation to evaluate the quality of our worldly workaday lives—to confront the question if they are worth all that much. In focusing upon the prospects of the next world it recognizes and highlights man's tendency to want more, to transcend the limitations of this sublunary world of ours, to aspire to more than life can offer. Pascal invites us to join the long line of Christians who hold that man is not only a citizen of the kingdom of nature but of the kingdom of grace as well.

2. The Wager Argument as a First Step

No doubt God must be expected to have a value framework akin to the human in this regard; at any rate, he, like us, would prefer to be loved for himself alone rather than for strictly prudential motives. Still, the journey toward disinterested love must make a start someplace. A human lover would certainly rather have that love reciprocated for his wealth or *beaux yeux* than not reciprocated at all. Wisely he recognizes that the love which begins in crass considerations of personal advantage, social conformity, or parental pressure may in time be purified by habit and the natural evolution of shared concerns into genuine communion and true affection. Here too the element of hope is present—the hope that an attachment born in an ambience of "unworthy" motives may ultimately change into something better and finer. Seeing that people are generally acute enough to sense this circumstance, there is no reason to think God to be unmindful of it.

William James scathingly condemned Pascal's argumentation:

> We feel that a faith . . . adopted willfully after such a mechanical calculation would lack the inner soul of faith's reality; and if we were ourselves in the place of the Deity, we should probably take particular pleasure in cutting off believers of this pattern from their infinite reward.[127]

Perhaps "if we were ourselves in the place of the Deity"—if we conceived God on our own model in these regards—all this might indeed be so. But, fortunately, the job has already been taken by someone who, on the Christian conception of the matter, at any rate, takes a very different approach. Mercifully, it is God who gets to play God, and not we humans. Pascal is committed to this idea—and it surely gets the point right.

By itself the prudential approach certainly falls far short of that full-bloodedly Christian position which calls for belief to rest not on self-interest but on a commitment to ideals—not on a calculation of advantage, but on genuine faith. The Wager argument is thus no more than a starting point. Its potential contribution is at most that which Pascal envisaged for it as a mere beginning for the process of Heart's enlightenment of Mind. The prudential orientation of the argument is only a point of departure on the journey toward a purer belief that moves from a hope for personal advantage toward a hope for the disinterested good. A faith based on prudential self-interest is not—cannot be—the end of the line. But Pascal sees it as a virtually inevitable place to begin for many or most men. To his mind what is unworthy is not his argumentation but rather its addressees. Man is unworthy. But it is, of course, man with whom we have to deal.

The aim of Pascal's Wager is to induce people to try the religious life. It appeals to prudence because in apologetics prudence is the best available instrument we have before taking the plunge, as it were. Later on, *ex post facto,* one can doubtless do more—and better.

William James criticized Pascal in the following terms:

> Surely Pascal's own personal belief . . . had far other springs, and this celebrated page of his is but an argument for others, a last desperate snatch at a weapon against the hardness of the unbelieving heart.[128]

James is quite right in the former regard, but his second point needs to be qualified. The Wager argument is not only a "last desperate snatch" but also an opening gun, an initiating move, the first step on a long and complex journey. He assures us that if we take that difficult first step and make the effort, all will come out well. But he realized—and realized that God realizes—that one must not be too fastidious in one's dealings with imperfect men. An appeal to prudence is not shameful but merely realistic.

It is (or should be) clear that there are various degrees of development in the religious life and very different heights to which it can attain. But the ascent must have a start. An appeal to interest of the Pascal's Wager type can at any rate set our feet on the right path. It can inaugurate that dynamic and developmental process through which the baser side of our nature can be won over by the nobler, which—initially—has little choice but to appeal to the former on its own terms.

Pascal is perfectly content to have his argument pivot on self-interest because, in the light of his apologetic aims, he views this as initially necessary to reach the sort of person whom he wants to persuade. There are also, of course, nonprudential grounds for belief, faith, and hope—reasons that are not crassly self-interested. And their inherent superiority is not to be denied. But one must walk before one can run—and one must make brittle iron before one can make firm steel. The less noble incentives to religious faith (or to morality, for that matter), are by no means contemptible in themselves precisely because they can provide helpful stepping-stones toward better things. It is not sensible for us to condemn fastidiously the humble helps along the journey's way. An ideology of all-or-nothing is neither very sensible nor very attractive.

The Wager argument is not intended (by Pascal at any rate) to provide for more than a first small step in the right direction. To motivate people effectively we must begin by meeting them where they are. And of course they are enmeshed in their own mundane affairs, devoted to self-advantage and self-interest. It is "men of the world," men of the stripe of the shady Chevalier de Méré, that typify the sort of person to whom Pascal addresses his book—and his Wager argument. The person whom Pascal has in view is exactly the one whose motivating inclinations are so trenchantly analyzed in the *Maxims* of La Rochefoucault—the person moved first and foremost by the prudential appreciation of self-interest. The Wager argument accordingly pivots on the appeal to personal advantage, to reach man's mind at that level of self-interested rationality which is its natural habitat. The self-serving cast of the argument is not a defect, but a condition of its adequacy for the job it is designed to achieve.

Is a calculating approach to belief wholly un-Christian? We read in Luke's gospel of Jesus saying:

> For which of you, intending to build a tower, sitteth not down first and counteth the cost, whether he have sufficient to finish it? . . . Or what king, going to make war against another king, sitteth not down first and consulteth whether he will be able with ten thousand to meet him that cometh against him with twenty thousand? . . . So likewise, whosoever he be of you that forsaketh not all that he hath, he cannot be my disciple. (Luke 14: 28–33)

Or again, in a more familiar passage from Matthew:

> For whosoever will save his life shall lose it: and whosoever will lose his life for my sake shall find it. For what is a man profited, if he shall gain the whole world, and lose his own soul? Or what shall a man give in exchange for his soul? (Matthew 16: 25–26)

It would seem that the founder of Christianity was himself prepared to invite people to bethink themselves of gains and losses and to compare the costs and benefits of discipleship with the costs and benefits of a worldly life. That being so, it is hardly fitting for Christian apologists to turn *plus royaliste que le roi* in condemning Pascal's invocation of exactly this same comparison.

The Wager argument can, without great violence, simply be read as a commentary on biblical passages of the preceding sort. What it does is to extend an invitation to contemplate the contrast between the real and the ideal orders and to consider the gulf between what we are and what we should try to be.

We will of course fail to bridge this gulf. In the religious life—as in the moral life and in the life of inquiry—we cannot attain perfection. Our task, however, is not to succeed to perfection, but to do our best—to make the effort. Authentic faith, comprehensive knowledge, genuine morality are all idealizations—aims that we cannot reach. They are idealizations that beckon us ever onward, and whose value lies not in the attainment but in the pursuit. The salient thing is not that we succeed to perfection, but that we keep trying—that we are not satisfied to sit contentedly where we are but feel impelled to persist, recognizing that even modest progress is worthwhile.

The Wager argument is thus only a beginning. It does not lead to the destination of the religious journey, but merely helps to provide a start. The journey has to begin somewhere. And with crassly mundane people a crassly mundane starting point is indicated. All the same, the Wager argument pivots on hope—and on a vision, however limited, of the good. It represents an expression of faith in the role of values in the scheme of things. And while the value at issue in the Wager argument is as such one of a rather low level—namely self-interest—Pascal is convinced that the matter neither should nor can stop there.

3. Heart's Journey toward Belief

Man is a creature of dual aspect, intellect and will, mind and heart. The intellect trades in information, the will in motivation. The intellect helps to provide direction, the will encouragement to action.

Pascal's argument begins in the recognition that cognitive reason can go only so far—that issues have to be faced and resolved in life's course that cannot be managed by evidential deliberations alone. And it insists on the need to recognize that some juncture will always be reached in the rational conduct of human affairs where probative rationality must yield way to normative rationality, where considerations of interest supplement considerations of evidence, and the questions "What sort of people do we want to be?" and "What do we want to make of ourselves?" become paramount.

The Wager argument appeals to the calculatingly self-interested rationality of Mind, slighting that side of the human spirit which Pascal characterized as Heart. And Heart takes its own view of the matter. It sees the argument as useful but limited—as no more than a convenient but unhappy concession to selfish Mind. It insists on the inadequacy of this entire probative approach to religious belief and demands a shift toward a God who *deserves* rather than *compels* allegiance. Pascal writes:

> The God of the Christians is not a god who is simply the author of mathematical truths or of the order of nature; that is the view of the pagans and Epicureans. He is not simply a god who exercises his providence . . . in bestowing upon those who worship him a long and happy life, as the Jews maintain. But the God of Abraham, the God of Isaac, the God of Jacob, the God of the Christians, is a God of love and consolation. He is a God who fills the head and souls of those whom he possesses, a God who makes them feel a profound sense of their wretchedness and of his infinite mercy, who unites himself with their inmost soul, filling it with humanity, joy, confidence, and love. (*Pensées,* 17/556)

Heart is an instrument of encouragement—providing incentives to do our utmost to make the best of a difficult situation in this world by looking hopefully toward a "something more" beyond.

The crux is that once man has been led to belief by Mind, Heart endeavors to *reeducate* him as to the nature of the God at issue. As Heart sees it, the God-conception of the Wager argument is a ladder to be abandoned once we have safely climbed it—a regrettable but largely unavoidable concession to the prudently self-interested crassness of Mind. Pascal's approach is predicated on the insight that the religious life—regardless of how deficient the grounds for which we initially enter upon it—has in itself the power to elevate and enlighten, increasingly leading its adherents toward authentic belief and genuine devotion.

"The heart has its order, and the intellect has its own, which is by way of principle and demonstrations."[129] Heart views with discontent the God of the philosophers, the God of demonstration who emerges at the end of a syllogism. Nor is Heart pleased with the jealous God Jehovah of the Old Testament—the God of intimidation, vengeance, and wrath. Moreover, Heart cannot rest satisfied with the God of the Wager argument, to whom we are led by inducements and bribery. Heart wants to change the terms of reference altogether. It wants to move beyond the God of the theologians and philosophers—the God of Mind, the God whose existence must needs be *argued* in some way or other.

*****

Pascal's distinction of "heart" from "mind" is of more than historical interest in its bearing on the controversy of science versus religion. The Bible tells us that "the heavens speak of God." But this is surely not because we learn about God in observing or studying or explaining the heavens. (In this regard much of the Western tradition of natural theology goes badly awry.) The heavens speak of God not because of their vastness or their regularity, but because they are awe-inspiring. God enters through the factor of appreciation, not through the factor of explanation.

For there indeed are two different orders of thought and deliberation, the order of *explanation* (Pascal's "*mind*") and the order of value apprehension, of *appreciation* (Pascal's "*heart*"). At the former level our concern is with the world's *modus operandi,* with understanding and explaining its furnishings and its laws. At the latter level we are concerned with apprehending the world's meaning—with matters of significance and worth and value, with what is beautiful and awesome and interesting in the world.

Already at the very outset of modern science Pascal

apprehended the distinctions needed to avert a clash between science and religion. Neither should meddle in the other's business. Different processes are at issue, and the theoretician cannot expect God to pluck his chestnuts from the fire—*non in scientia recurrere est ad deum,* to put it in a somewhat medieval way. It is simply inappropriate to see God as an instrumentality of explanation—as having a role in scientific deliberations. The proper place for the conception of God is our thought in relation to the order of appreciation, not in relation to the order of explanation. And one no more learns about the value of the world by examining it scientifically than one can learn about the value of a banknote by examining it scientifically. (Like all analogies, this one is imperfect. The value of the paper lies in the eyes of its beholders; that of the world lies in the object itself. That is because monetary value is one thing, ontological value another.)

"I believe in one God, maker of heaven and earth" the Nicene Creed proclaims. But *in what sense* is God the "maker" of the universe?

Well—not in the sense that God is part of the world's causal machinery, that we can draw inferences about him from the facts of the world's *modus operandi* that emerge in the course of the scientific study of nature.

God is the world's maker in the minimal sense that if he weren't there, then it couldn't be there: it wouldn't exist if he didn't. But this is something that allows him to remain very much in the background of the story of nature. No doubt he works through the scientific facts: they are as they are because he wants them that way. But that doesn't make him part of the order of scientific fact. And it doesn't prevent the order from being self-sustained in the sphere of causal explanation. As such, the causal order does not point to something transcendent that lies beyond. The task of "natural theology"—of drawing inferences about God's nature from the order of nature by somehow linking him up with the world's causal order—is a hopeless proposition.

God's connection with the world is not a *causal* one: he is not a "maker" in *that* way. He "stands in back" of the causal order in some sense but is not part of it.

The author of nature is no more part of the story of nature than is the author of a book a part of its story. Consider an epic poem like the *Iliad.* Essentially nothing can be deduced about its authorship from its content. Did it even have an author, or did it "just grow." No secure inference can be drawn from the work by itself to the nature (or even the existence) of an author. Its status as a "work" is not inherent in the work itself. (This analogy is also imperfect. One immense difference is that we ourselves are part of the world's story. And so we are in a position to make that "leap of faith" to the assured confidence that it is a *meaningful* story. But this is not something we can read off from a scientific account of the causal order of things.)

The writings of God's hand are not found on the pages of the "great book of nature" which natural science laboriously spells out for us. They are inscribed on the hearts of men. It is not the mind's work in science that informs us about the ways of God, but the heart's receptivity to his messages.

Neither need scientific knowledge engender faith nor will belief in God enhance our ability to understand or explain the world. What such belief does accomplish is to enhance our ability to appreciate the world and to feel at home in it—to see it as a fundamentally friendly rather than hostile place. (If the world picture of science were alone at our disposal, those vast emptinesses would frighten us.)

To say that we do not find God in or through (the study of) nature is not, of course, to deny God. It is simply to recognize that reality is larger than nature, that there is not only a kingdom of nature but also a kingdom of grace.

To be sure, if nature were suitably different, we would not think of it as an expression of divine goodness. If the shape of this *A* were duly different, we would not think of it as a letter, as an expression of human meaning. But that does not mean that God *causes* the world any more than that the meaning *causes* the letter. It is this noncausal, "symbolic" nature of issues of meaning and value that puts them outside the scientific domain. To be sure, man is a creature of nature, and nature must be such as to make his access to God possible—to *permit* it, and perhaps even to *facilitate* it. (That, after all, is the object of the Wager argument, to lead people to God through an appeal to their fundamentally base nature.) There cannot be a complete disconnection between the realms of knowledge and valuation. The world, as science depicts it, must be capable of a sympathetic resonance with the sphere of value. But that does not mean that it is through nature and mind that we attain God. We reach him through grace and heart—he comes to meet us halfway.

The biblical God is not at the disposal of mind—he is not a creature of theory, of rational inference or inductive projection from observational experience. He is a literally *supernatural* being whom we do not discover by scientific inquiry but are able to recognize in and through our *evaluative* experience—to whom we gain access through heart rather than mind. He is not an instrument of explanation but a source of value—the God of Heart rather than Mind.

*****

The rationalist theologians ask: How is God to be thought of if this conception is to be able to satisfy Mind (= the calculatingly rational side of man) that belief in him is epistemically warranted? That just is not Heart's way at all. Heart sees the key question as this: If it does turn out—perhaps wholly against our expectations, beliefs, inclinations, and even wishes—that God exists, *what sort of God would we welcome having*? If we could have God as we want him, what sort of God would we really want?

The answer here is not all that difficult. The sort of God we would want is the sort of God who could accept (love, forgive, embrace) us.

Well—perhaps not *all* of us. Groucho Marx said, "I don't care to belong to any social organization that would accept me as a member." Similarly, perhaps, some of us might feel: "I wouldn't want to believe in a God with standards low enough to accept (love, forgive) people like me" (or perhaps, rather, "people like *X*"). No doubt some of us relish wrapping the mantle of our unworthiness about ourselves—or about our fellows, for that matter. But that again is Mind speaking. Heart's task is precisely to reeducate us—to lead us to see ourselves not as *deserving* of God's love, but nevertheless as fully *eligible* for it. Heart tries to get us to grasp the possibility of *grace*—to bring us into a situation where faith, hope, and charity begin to warm the chilled interior of our soul.

If the argumentation of Pascal's Wager is viewed in this light, certain consequences follow for the *kind* of God at issue. It is not the God of the philosophers, the God found at the end of a syllogism, the God of scholastic demonstration—of Anselm's Ontological Argument and of St. Thomas' Third Way. It is not a God whose existence can be demonstrated by abstract reasonings—who can be caught within the premises of an argument and necessitated as a conclusion. Rather, it is a God of hope, a God of encouragement and comfort—the aspiration and consolation of a weak creature seeking to make its way amidst the shoals and narrows of a difficult world. From our human vantage point in the epistemic dispensation, this God is more a matter of "wishful thinking" than of accomplished demonstration—a hope rather than a *fait accompli.* (Of course, whether such a God accords with one's religious convictions is something everyone must judge for himself.)

Heart's job, then, is the great civilizing mission of gradual transformation—of guiding us along the long and often difficult road of spiritual development. Mind may well be pressed into service to get us started: the Wager argument has its place. But its place is no more than a starting point for launching the journey on its way. "It is Heart that experiences God, and not Reason. This, then, is faith: God perceived by the heart—and not by reason."[130]

The religious life is clearly a matter of development, evolution, and growth; it is a spiritual journey, an ascent. It can proceed on many levels: the plane of prudential self-interest, the plane of morality, and ultimately also the plane of a more deeply developed spirituality. The utility and appropriateness of prudential argumentation lies in its affording a starting point even at a crass, personal, self-interested level—a beginning that can and ultimately should be developed at higher levels of a more elevated spirituality.

Pascal thus envisages a certain division of labor. Mind moves us toward the sort of God we are rationally well advised to believe in. The work of Heart is to lead us beyond this point, to cut the ropes that tie us to the moorings of self-concern and self-interest. Heart urges us toward the sort of God we *want to* believe in—the sort of God whose existence we would welcome but dare not expect. It does not allow man to rest content with the God of the theoreticians who satisfies Mind but enjoins a faith in the sort of God who *deserves* rather than *requires* belief, and who responds with open-endedly generous receptiveness to even the smallest, most halting, and imperfect attempt to reach out toward him.

4. Final Considerations

Is such a faith irrational? Not at all. For, as Pascal sees it, rationality as such is something comprehensive, something that goes well beyond narrowly calculating self-interest. The broader realm of rationality encompasses interests of the most complex and diverse character, and not prudential advantage alone. Man has not only "material" (welfare-oriented) interests but also "higher" interests in the role of values in reality's scheme of things. Rationality embraces not only the rationality of Mind but the rationality of Heart as well. Mind does not have the corner on the market of reason: "The Heart has its reasons of which Mind knows nothing."[131] The Wager argument is an expression of this fact: an expression, to be sure, not of demonstrated *knowledge* but of rationalized *hope*—a hope that reality is congenial to the deepest aspirations and interests of man.

Notes

Preface

1. These editions, all published in Paris, were issued in 1952 (Éditions de Luxemburg), 1962 (Éditions de Seuil), and 1963 (in the series *L'Intégrale* by the same publisher), and in a version accompanied by a photographic reproduction of Pascal's original manuscript, published in 1962 by Libraires Associés in commemoration of the tercentenary of Pascal's death.

I. Pascal's Turning

2. The passage is numbered as section 343 in Lafuma's Delmas edition of 1952 and is numbered 233 in Léon Brunschvicg's earlier edition (Paris: Hachette, 1914). The original text is now in the Bibliothèque Nationale in Paris. A photograph of the MS is given in Georges Brunet, *Le Pari de Pascal* (Paris, 1956), in Lafuma's 1962 tercentenary edition, and in Henri Gouhier, *Blaise Pascal: Commentaires* (Paris, 1971). There has been much indecisive speculation regarding the time and circumstances of this draft.
time and circumstances of this draft.

3. Principal John Tulloch, *Pascal* (Edinburgh and London, 1878), p. 192. He insists that "it is impossible to defend this essay on any principle of sound philosophy" and maintains that the argument "was hardly worthy of Pascal" (p. 193).

4. Terence Penelhum, *God and Scepticism* (Dordrecht, Boston,

Lancaster, 1983); this book is virtually unique in treating the argument with respect.

5. René Descartes, *Meditations on First Philosophy,* no. 4. Cf. *Descartes: Philosophical Writings,* tr. by E. Anscombe and P. T. Geach (London, 1954), p. 93.

6. *Pensées,* 381/543. While this passage appears in all editions of the *Pensées* remote from the Wager discussion, it is one of four jottings written on the same paper used by Pascal for the "*infini-rien*" fragment. See Georges Brunet, *Le Pari de Pascal* (Paris, 1956), pp. 48–51.

7. *Pensées,* 727/280.

8. *Pensées,* 343/233. To "incapable of knowing" here, we must add "by way of human inquiring reason." Knowledge by way of *experience* is not to be precluded. After the miracle of the Holy Thorn in 1654, Pascal adopted the motto *Scio cui credidi,* "I (now) know him in whom I (heretofore merely) believed." See H. F. Stewart, "Blaise Pascal," *Proceedings of the British Academy,* vol. 28 (1942), pp. 196–215 (see p. 203).

9. Michel de Montaigne, "Apologie de Raimond Sebond" in P. Villey (ed.), *Les Essais de Michel de Montaigne,* tome 2 (Paris, 1922), pp. 367–71.

10. Pascal's supposition of an equal chance of gain and loss is simply illustrative. It is emphatically not an invocation of the Laplacian principle of indifference to establish equiprobability between the two possibilities of God's existence and God's nonexistence. The particular value at issue is in fact entirely irrelevant to the outcome of the argument. (Compare notes 18, 19, and 30 below.)

11. The third session of the Vatican Council of 1869–70 was to reiterate this long-standing rejection in the canon *De Revelatione*: "If anyone says that one true God, our creator and Lord, cannot be known for certain by the natural light of human reason through the things which are made: let him be cast out of the Church." (Denzinger, sect. 1806)

12. Indeed, reason is man's noblest feature; though but a reed, he is a *thinking* reed. *Pensées,* 391/347. Man's dignity and greatness consists in thought (ibid., 126/146 and 232–33/365–66).

13. Compare *Pensées* 9/276. For Pascal's many-faceted conception of rational demonstration see chap. 1, "Proof and Proofs," in Hugh M. Davidson, *The Origins of Certainty: Means and Meanings in Pascal's Pensées* (Chicago and London, 1979). Regarding that section of the theological tradition which urged not that reason is dispensable, but

(with Pascal) that faith must bring grist to reason's mill before reason can accomplish any useful work in theology, see Richard H. Popkin, *The History of Skepticism from Erasmus to Spinoza* (Berkeley and Los Angeles, 1979).

14. See William James, *The Will to Believe and Other Essays in Popular Philosophy* (New York and London, 1896), pp. 2–3. The issues that arise here are usefully canvassed in Marcus G. Singer, "The Pragmatic Use of Language and the Will to Believe," *American Philosophical Quarterly,* vol. 8 (1971), pp. 24–34, and in Richard M. Gale, "William James and the Ethics of Belief," ibid., vol. 17 (1980), pp. 1–14.

15. *Pensées,* sect. 343/233. This is the core of Pascal's skepticism: in this apologetic domain we are in a terrain where theoretical, inquiring reason (Kant's "speculative" reason) cannot resolve our questions by providing properly authenticated knowledge.

16. This idea is foreshadowed in the *Mémorial* Pascal wrote concerning the inspirational religious experience he had on the night of November 23, 1654: "Total submission to Jesus Christ and my director/Everlasting joy in return for one day's effort on earth." (The passage may, however, be a later addendum.)

17. This model reflects the situation as described in the notes on pp. 147–50 of L. Brunschvicg's edition of the *Pensées.*

18. "But then we are brought back to our original and persistent question: Are the existence and the non-existence of God equally balanced in probability as far as our knowledge goes—like the two sides of a newly minted coin?" Monroe and Elizabeth Beardsley, *Philosophical Thinking: An Introduction* (New York, 1965), p. 140.

19. On this point our analysis differs decisively from that of Ian Hacking, who sees this section of the *infini-rien* discussion as developing a further "argument for dominating expectation," because the earlier argument somehow depends on the obviously problematic supposition that the probability of God's existence is one-half. See his essay "The Logic of Pascal's Wager," *American Philosophical Quarterly,* vol. 9 (1972), pp. 186–92 (see p. 189). The same discussion recurs in *The Emergence of Probability* (Cambridge, 1975), pp. 63–72. (Compare notes 11 and 30.)

20. This is what nonzero subjective probability comes to here: accepting with substantial confidence that God may possibly exist. It is *not* a matter of accepting with low confidence that God does in fact exist.

21. "[W]e must not lose sight of the fact that we are automatic

as well as intelligent beings. . . . Proofs only convince the mind. Custom is for us the strongest and most readily accepted proof; it sways the automatic, which bears the unthinking mind along with it." (*Pensées,* 7/252). On Pascal's view of the "automatic" dimension of belief and in the aspect of man as "*la machine*" see chap. 3, "Fixation of Belief" of Hugh M. Davidson, *The Origins of Certainty* (Chicago and London, 1979).

22. *Pensées,* 343/233. Terence Penelhum makes an important point in this connection. The task of those religious practices Pascal recommends is to *engender* faith. He is not under the illusion that they *constitute* it:

> Pascal does not say that the practices which one enters in pursuit of faith themselves constitute faith. They are merely those activities that someone who *has* faith engages in, and he proposes that someone who wishes to be of their number should engage in them as well in order to acquire it. The enterprise he proposes is only successful if real faith actually ensues. Believing as he does that faith is a gift of grace, he implies that someone seeking to acquire it may be granted it if he makes efforts to remove some of its obstacles. It seems to me theologically unacceptable for Christian thinkers to insist against him that someone wanting faith, even for prudential reasons, would be denied it by God. (*God and Scepticism* [Dordrecht, Boston, Lancaster, 1983], pp. 72–77.)

23. David Hume, *A Treatise of Human Nature,* appendix; p. 624 in the edition by L. A Selby-Bigge (Oxford, 1888).

24. R. G. Swinburne, "The Christian Wager," *Religious Studies,* vol. 4 (1969), pp. 217–28 (see p. 222). That our beliefs are not within our control is argued at length in Bernard Williams, "Deciding to Believe," in *Problems of the Self* (Cambridge, 1973), pp. 136–51. That we can embark on courses of action that are likely to induce certain beliefs is persuasively maintained H. H. Price, "Belief and Will," *Proceedings of the Aristotelian Society,* Supplementary Volume 28 (London, 1954), pp. 1–26.

25. R. G. Swinburne, "The Christian Wager," *Religious Studies,* vol. 4 (1969), pp. 217–28 (see p. 220).

26. *Pensées,* 343/233 *ad fin.*

27. For Silhon see chap. 8 of Richard Popkin, *The History of Scepticism from Erasmus to Spinoza* (Berkeley and Los Angeles, 1979).

28. Popkin, ibid., p. 173.

29. Ian Hacking, *The Emergence of Probability* (Cambridge, 1975), p. 66.

30. Many writers object that the Wager argument is defective because it supposedly requires Pascal to have recourse to a Laplacian principle of indifference in establishing that the existence of God is a possibility of nonzero probability. See, for example:

James Cargile, "Pascal's Wager," *Philosophy,* vol. 41 (1966), pp. 250–57 (see p. 255).

Peter C. Dalton, "Pascal's Wager," *The Southern Journal of Philosophy,* vol. 13 (1975), pp. 31–46 (see p. 40).

But this criticism misfires. The argument neither can nor endeavors to convince those who do not see God's existence as a *real possibility.* Someone for whom the Christian God is a dead hypothesis (in William James's sense) is going to be untouched by Pascal's Wager.

31. These issues are treated in greater detail in the author's *Scepticism* (Oxford, 1980).

32. See M. L. Goldman, "Le Pari, est-il ecrit 'Pour le libertin'?" in *Blaise Pascal: L'Homme et l'oeuvre* (Paris, 1956; Cahiers de Royaumont), sect. 4. Here it is maintained that the Wager argument is aimed not at the skeptic who is *satisfied* with life in this world, but at those who are alive to the misery of man's lot and the anguish of the human condition. As Pascal sees it, however, this includes virtually everybody, since however smug and self-sufficient we may be, everyone has *some* share of existential *Angst,* of deep-rooted doubt about the ultimate value of what life in this world offers to man, seeing that the inevitable terminus of all our efforts and strivings is the grave.

33. "There are three sources of belief: reason, custom and inspiration. The Christian religion . . . does not acknowledge as her true children those who believe without inspiration. Not that she excludes reason and custom. On the contrary, the mind must be opened to proofs, must be strengthened by custom, and humbly submit to inspiration, which alone can produce a true and salutary effect." (*Pensées,* 396/245)

34. Thomas More, "The Supplication of Soules" in *The Workes of Sir Thomas More* (London, 1557), p. 329; quoted in John K. Ryan, "The Argument of the Wager in Pascal and Others," *The New Scholasticism,* vol. 19 (1945), pp. 233–350 (see p. 328).

35. Arnobius, *Against the Heathen (Adversus gentes),* II, 3–4; *Ante-Nicine Fathers,* tr. by H. Bryce and H. Campbell (New York,

1907), vol. 5, p. 434. Pierre Bayle already remarked on the kinship of Pascal's line of thought with that of Arnobius. For a discussion of similar parallels see Jules Lachelier, "Notes sur le pari de Pascal" appended to his *Du Fondement de l'induction* (Paris, 1907), pp. 175–208, and Louis Blanchet, "L'Attitude réligieuse des Jesuites et les sources du pari de Pascal," *Revue de métaphysique et de morale,* vol. 24 (1919), pp. 477-516 and 617–47. Precursors of Pascal are also discussed in Georges Brunet, *Le Pari de Pascal* (Paris, 1956), p. 62. For precedents in Islamic philosophical theology see Miguel Asin Palacios, *Los Precedentes Musulmanes del Pari de Pascal* (Santander, 1921). Such precedents, however, only relate to the general (and old) idea of using prudence as a prop of faith. The characteristic features of the Wager argument in its reliance on probability and decision theory are altogether new. Thus Antony Flew is quite wrong in saying apropos of Asin Palacios that "Scholarship has now apparently traced the origin of the (Wager) argument back to the Islamic apologist Algazel" ("Is Pascal's Wager the Only Safe Bet?" *The Rationalist Annual,* vol. 76 (1960), pp. 21–25 [see p. 21]).

36. On Pascal's contribution to the theory of probability see Isaac Todhunter, *A History of the Mathematical Theory of Probability* (London and Cambridge, 1865) and Oystein Ore, "Pascal and the Origination of Probability Theory," *American Mathematical Monthly,* vol. 67 (1960), pp. 409–19. See also Jean Mesnard, *Pascal et les Roannez* (Bruges, 1965). Todhunter and Ore do not, however, take any notice of the Wager argument. But it is treated at length in Ian Hacking, *The Emergence of Probability* (Cambridge, 1975).

37. John Locke, *Essay Concerning Human Understanding,* bk. II, chap. 21, sect. 70.

38. John K. Ryan, "The Argument of the Wager in Pascal and Others," *New Scholasticism,* vol. 19 (1945), pp. 233–50 (see p. 247).

39. Antony Flew, "Is Pascal's Wager the Only Safe Bet?" *The Rationalist Annual,* vol. 76 (1960), pp. 21–25 (see pp. 24–25); reprinted in revised form in *God, Freedom, and Immortality* (Buffalo, 1984), pp. 61–68 (see p. 68).

40. For an informative account of the basic issues regarding various modes of probability and their uses see Wesley C. Salmon, *The Foundations of Scientific Inference* (Pittsburgh, 1967).

41. P. S. de Laplace, *Essaie philosophique sur les probabilités,* in *Oeuvres,* vol. 11 (Paris, 1886); *A Philosophical Essay on Probabilities,* tr. by E. W. Truscott and F. L. Emory (New York, 1948), see chap.

11, pp. 109–25.

42. This disagrees with the view of Ian Hacking, who dismissively comments: "Curiously, Laplace takes . . . (his argument) to refute Pascal." ("The Logic of Pascal's Wager," *American Philosophical Quarterly*, vol. 9 (1972), pp. 186–92 (see p. 192).) If Laplace's point were correct and his analysis did indeed establish that p, the probability that the Christian God exists, were zero, then Pascal's argument would indeed be in difficulty.

43. Its being reported by a highly unreliable source tells us effectively nothing about the probability of the claimed fact itself. An unreliable source is of course not one that is *contra-indicative* (i.e., that reliably speaks falsehood), but one that is *irresponsible*—that speaks truth and falsehood more or less randomly. For such a source we only know that the proportion of (relevantly comparable) cases where it "knows what it is talking about" (k) is small. Accrodingly, the *a posteriori* probability that a statement p (of the relevant class) that is attested by our source is true is:

$$k \cdot 1 + (1 - k) \cdot \mathrm{pr}(p) = \mathrm{pr}(p) + k \cdot \mathrm{pr}(\text{not-}p).$$

(We suppose the source is right within the range of its knowledge, and only meets with randomly average success elsewhere.) From the fact that k is small we can thus infer no more than our source's inability to augment the *a priori* probability of its statements by any substantial amount.

44. P. S. de Laplace, *A Philosophical Essay on Probabilities*, chap. 11, pp. 109–25 (see esp. pp. 120–22).

45. For Gataker (1574–1654) see the DNB, vol. 21 (London, 1919; 2nd. ed., 1927).

46. F. M. A. de Voltaire, "Remarques sur les Pensées de M. Pascal." Letter XXV (1728) of *Lettres philosophiques par M. de V**** (Amsterdam, 1734). For a reprint and critical study see Gustave Larson (ed.), *Voltaire: Lettres philosophiques*, 2 vols. (Paris, 1916 [3rd ed. 1929] and 1917).

47. H. F. Stewart, "Blaise Pascal," *Proceedings of the British Academy*, vol. 28 (1942), pp. 196–215 (see p. 204). For Méré's role in the origins of probability theory see Ian Hacking, *The Emergence of Probability* (Cambridge, 1975).

48. Regarding the pragmatism of the Middle Academy see Charlotte L. Stough, *Greek Skepticism* (Berkeley and Los Angeles, 1968), especially pp. 125–50 ff.

49. Kant's discussion of theological issues in the "Canon of Pure Reason" section of the first *Critique* is clearly based on Pascal—no doubt via intermediaries. There is, to be sure, a parting of the ways between Pascal and Kant on the issue of the relation of faith and morality. Kant in effect transposed the traditional inference

We do believe in God

Therefore: We ought to be moral

into an inverted form

We ought to be moral

Therefore: We should believe in God

Pascal's apologetic purposes lead him to sever the linkage between faith and morality—at any rate in the first instance—and to pivot his appeal entirely on the self-interest of sinful and imperfect man.

50. Kant, *Critique of Pure Reason,* A 828-29 = B857-58.

51. To be sure, James's pragmatism has a moral dimension; it is oriented not at what is factually desired but at what is normatively desirable.

52. William James, *The Will to Believe and Other Essays in Popular Philosophy* (New York and London, 1896), p. 11. For a helpful discussion of James's defense of faith, one that quite properly highlights its practical and moral dimension, see Richard M. Gale, "William James and the Ethics of Belief," *American Philosophical Quarterly,* vol. 17 (1980), pp. 1–14.

53. J. L. Mackie speaks of "Pascal's view that when speculative reason cannot decide, self-seeking practical reason can act as a tie-breaker." (*The Miracle of Theism* [Oxford, 1982], p. 209.) This gets Pascal quite wrong, conflating his position with that of William James.

54. Hans Küng, *Does God Exist?* (London, 1980). Originally published in German, *Existiert Gott?* (Munich, 1978). All references here are to the English version.

II. The Epistemology of Pragmatic Beliefs

55. William James, *The Will to Believe and Other Essays in Popular Philosophy* (New York, 1896), pp. 5–6.

56. Jean Mesnard, *Pascal: His Life and Works,* tr. by G. S. Fraser

(London, 1952), pp. 156–57.

57. James Boswell, *The Life of Samuel Johnson,* vol. 1, ed. by Arnold Glover (London, 1925), p. 419.

58. Kant, *Critique of Pure Reason,* A829 = B857.

59. The wording "no *decisive* reason," rather than "no *good* reason," is significant here. Belief can be pragmatically warranted even in the face of counterevidence. (I may be entitled to believe my friend's protestation of innocence even when matters look bad.)

60. The thesis that well-evidentiated beliefs are likely to be true has been taking some pretty hard knocks in the tradition of philosophy of science that follows the lead of K. R. Popper and Thomas Kuhn.

61. Compare Roderick Chisholm, *Theory of Knowledge,* 2nd ed. (Englewood Cliffs, 1979), p. 14.

62. The presently operative distinction between *evidential* and *prudential* (or *pragmatic*) reasons runs parallel to that between *evidential* and *beneficial* reasons drawn in Michel Martin's interesting paper, "On Four Critiques of Pascal's Wager" in *Sophia,* vol. 14 (1975), pp. 1–11. Martin, however, thinks that "Pascal's argument can be interpreted as showing that practically any evidential reason is outweighed by a beneficial reason" (p. 2). Our view, however, is that Pascal's recourse to "beneficial reasons" is a matter of evidential gap filling, so that beneficial considerations cannot *override* but only *supplement* evidential considerations. In this light Pascal's evidential skepticism in apologetic matters comes to be seen as a necessary prerequisite of the Wager argument.

63. Hume, *Enquiry Concerning Human Understanding,* sect. 10, pt. 2.

64. Compare H. H. Price, *Belief* (London, 1969).

65. J. L. Mackie, *The Miracle of Theism* (Oxford, 1982), p. 202.

66. Cf. chapter 11, "Belief without Reason" in J. L. Mackie, *The Miracle of Theism* (Oxford, 1982), pp. 199–203.

67. W. K. Clifford, "The Ethics of Belief" in *Lectures and Essays* (London, 1879; 2nd ed., 1886).

68. The point is not that self-deception can never have any value (for example, in enabling us to avert the horror of impending doom, if only for a little while). Rather, since deception is at issue, the justification it yields is (*ex hypothesi*) not related to informative gap filling. Its bearing is now *purely* practical and nowise cognitive, since "we know better."

69. There might be circumstances where this is appropriate. Sometimes we do indeed let the interest of the community establish a rationale for setting evidence aside. (Think of "excluded evidence" in legal situations of evidential admissibility.) Something like this also occurs when we allow trust in a friend to prevail over potentially damaging evidence: "I acknowledge that the evidence points to his guilt, but I cannot believe it of him."

70. We are too "rational" merely to be content "to act as though" we believed. For a rational creature cannot be satisfied as such while his actions are out of alignment with what he *really* believes to be efficient in conducing to his ends.

71. Note that "The evidence indicates that I probably cannot do *A*, but I'm sure I can do it" is coherent, but "The evidence establishes that I cannot do *A*, but I'm sure I can" is not.

72. W. K. Clifford, "The Ethics of Belief" in *Lectures and Essays,* ed. by L. Stephen and F. Pollock (London, 1879), p. 50.

73. William James, *The Will to Believe and Other Essays in Popular Philosophy* (New York, 1896), pp. 96–97.

74. G. W. Leibniz, *Die philosophischen Schriften,* ed. by C. I. Gerhardt (Berlin, 1875–90), vol. 3 (1887), p. 621.

75. Antony Flew, *God and Philosophy* (New York, 1966), p. 182. Cf. also "Is Pascal's Wager the Only Safe Bet?" in *God, Freedom, and Immortality* (Buffalo, 1984), pp. 62–68.

76. Compare W. K. Clifford:

> In like manner, if I let myself believe anything on insufficient evidence . . . [then] the damage to society is not merely that it should believe wrong things, though that is great enough, but that it should become credulous, and lose the habit of testing things and inquiring into them; for then it must sink back into savagery. (*The Ethics of Belief* p. 50).

77. James Cargile, "Pascal's Wager," *Philosophy,* vol. 41 (1966), pp. 250–57 (see p. 255).

78. To say nothing, of course, of the question of whether *E* must be a reasonable end.

79. On self-deception see Herbert Fingarette, *Self-Deception* (London, 1969). Cf. also Amelie Rorty, "Belief and Self-Deception," *Inquiry* vol. 15 (1972), pp. 387–410; and David Pears, "Freud, Sartre, and Self-Deception" in *Freud,* ed. by R. Wollheim (New York, 1974), pp. 97–112.

80. R. Robinson, *An Atheist's Values* (Oxford, 1964; paperback, 1975), p. 117.

81. For Jurieu see H. M. Baird, *The Huguenots and the Revocation of the Edict of Nantes* (London, 1895).

82. See the interesting discussion in the final chapter in "Belief, Bias and Ideology" in Jon Elster, *Sour Grapes* (Cambridge, 1983).

83. R. Nisbet and L. Ross, *Human Inference: Strategies and Shortcomings of Social Judgment* (Englewood Cliffs, 1980), p. 271. Note that there is room for doubt that self-deception is actually going on here. Is "My prospects of hitting *this* ball are good" really incompatible with "In the past I've only managed to hit 20 percent of the balls"? (Compare footnote 71 above.)

84. On this theme see the discussions of Fingarette and Pears cited in note 79 above.

85. See the author's *Induction* (Oxford, 1980).

86. See the author's *Scepticism* (Oxford, 1980) for a discussion of this point and its ramifications.

87. William Kingdom Clifford, *Lectures and Essays,* ed. by L. Stephen and F. Pollock (London, 1879; 2nd ed. 1886); originally published in the *Contemporary Review,* vol. 30 (1877), pp. 42–54. In actual fact Clifford did not adhere to this hyperbolic standard throughout his epistemology. Rejecting the prospect of certainty in the area of *scientific* knowledge, he took the line that man's scientific "knowledge" of nature rests on various principles that are not in the final analysis justified on cognitive grounds at all but must be accounted for in terms of natural selection. The principle of the uniformity of nature is a prime example, and "Nature is selecting for survival those individuals and races who act as if she were uniform; and hence the gradual spread of that belief over the civilized world." (*The Common Sense of the Exact Sciences* [London, 1885], p. 209.)

88. James wrote, "*We must know the truth; and we must avoid error* . . . are two separable laws. . . . We may regard the chase for truth as paramount . . . or we may, on the other hand, treat the avoidance of error as more imperative, and let truth take its chance." (*The Will to Believe and Other Essays in Popular Philosophy* [New York, 1896], pp. 17–18.) The situation in ethics as between a negative morality ("Avoid evil!") and a positive morality ("Promote good!") is of course a parallel. For a useful outline of the James-Clifford controversy and its background see Peter Kauber, "The Foundations of James' Ethics of Belief," *Ethics,* vol. 84 (1974), pp.

151–66, where the relevant issues are set out and further references to the literature are given.

89. For a fuller discussion of these issues see chap. 8 of the author's *Scepticism* (Oxford, 1980), and chap. 10 of *Empirical Inquiry* (London, 1982).

90. R. G. Swinburne, "The Christian Wager," *Religion Studies,* vol. 4 (1969), pp. 217–28.

91. William James, *The Will to Believe and Other Essays in Popular Philosophy* (New York, 1896), pp. 27–28.

92. H. H. Price has put the key point at issue here very well:

> But "safety first" is not a good motto, however tempting it may be to some philosophers. The end we seek to achieve is to acquire as many correct beliefs as possible on as many subjects as possible. No one of us is likely to achieve this end if he resolves to reject the evidence of testimony, and contents himself with what he can know, or have reason to believe, on the evidence of his own first-hand experience alone. It cannot be denied that if someone follows the policy of accepting the testimony of others unless or until he has specific reason for doubting it, the results will not be all that he might wish. Some of the beliefs which he will thereby acquire will be totally incorrect, and others partly incorrect. In this sense, the policy is certainly a risky one. . . but it is reasonable to take this risk, and unreasonable not to take it. If we refuse to take it, we have no prospect of getting answers, not even the most tentative ones, for many of the questions which interest us. (H. H. Price, *Belief* [London, 1969], p. 128.)

III. Practical Reasoning in Theology

93. *Pensées,* 449/585.

94. Compare also *Pensées,* sect. 11/194. If God were not hidden, self-interest would be not merely the starting point of faith but its constant companion.

95. Of course, man would presumably be better off it it eventuated that *B* & *R*. But we may suppose that he willfully views this security as being bought at too high a price given that he would, as per sect. 1 above, "prefer" that God simply did not exist.

96. For an interesting discussion see Steven J. Brams, "Mathematics and Theology: Game-Theoretic Implications of God's Omni-

science," *Mathematics Magazine*, vol. 53 (1980), pp. 277–82.

97. This distinction runs parallel to Leibniz's distinction between the "antecedent choice" (*voluntas antecedens*) of what one would take if no counterconsiderations entered into it, and the "consequent choice" (*voluntas consequens*) of what one selects when everything is said and done, and one must accept the circumstantially optimal resolution that is compatible with one's other wishes.

98. To be sure, it is sometimes said that Pascal's Wager argument is designed to frighten man off from the prospect of disbelief by the threat of hellfire. Thus Antony Flew flatly insists that "it is part of the very framework of Pascal's Wager that it is, or would be, part of God's arrangements that anyone who fails to take the steps required for safety incurs the penalty of agony eternal." ("Is Pascal's Wager the Only Safe Bet?" in *God, Freedom, and Immortality* [Buffalo, 1984], p. 64.) See also Bernard Williams, *Moral Luck* (Cambridge, 1981), p. 98. But this is simply a mistake. The Wager argument takes the *via positiva* of looking to God's benevolence rather than to his wrath, and Pascal is explicit in insisting that "to instill it (belief) into the mind and heart by means of force and threats is not to instil religion, but terror" (*Pensées,* 387/185). The Wager discussion, however, is oriented positively to the prospect of benefits, not negatively to the prospect of punishment, numberless expositions to the contrary notwithstanding. To be sure, Pascal does indeed say that the unbeliever confronts "*l'horrible nécessité d'être éternellement ou anéanti* (if he is right) *ou malheureux* (if he is not)" (*Pensées,* 12/195). But for the sophisticates whose God-conception is determinative the eternal misery at issue here (and at 11/194) is presumably that of a regret at loss rather than torment by Satan's helpers in a Breughelian underworld.

99. This circumstance that the more forgiving one thinks God to be, the weaker the Pascalian expectation-argument for believing in him, has been commented on by several writers. See, for example, P. T. Landsberg, "Gambling on God," *Mind,* vol. 80 (1971), pp. 100–4.

100. Denis Diderot, *Pensées philosophiques,* sect. 59, in *Oeuvres,* ed. by J. Assezat (Paris, 1875–77), vol. 1, p. 167. Or again: "*Qui ne voit—dice—que Mahomet pouvait addresser la même raisonnement à eux qu' il voulait convertir?*" (Adolfo Garnier, *Larousse: Grand dictionnaire,* s.v. Pari.) This criticism is repeated time and again, generally without any acknowledgment of priority.

101. Pascal himself certainly worries about this fact that, to all appearances, people are simply *born* into a religion. See *Pensées*, 429/615.

102. William James, *The Will to Believe and Other Essays in Popular Philosophy* (New York and London, 1896), pp. 3ff.

103. This was clearly seen by one of Pascal's earlier editors:

> *Quant à ceux qui objectent à Pascal que son argument servirait à toutes les religions, et que Mahomet pourrait parler comme il parle, ils ne songent pas que Pascal n' accorderait pas que la raison soit embarrassée de decider sur Mahomet: la fausseté de la religion du Prophète lui est tout d'abord évidente. Il n' y à donc la ni calcul à faire, ni pari.* (E. Havet [ed.], *Pascal, Pensées* [Paris 1852], p. 185n.)

104. Compare the discussion of essentially this same situation in Michel Martin, "On Four Critiques of Pascal's Wager," *Sophia*, vol. 14 (1975), pp. 1–11 (see pp. 5–7).

105. See the author's *Risk* (Washington, 1983) for an analysis of the decision strategies at issue.

106. Compare George Schlesinger, *Religion and Scientific Method* (Dordrecht and Boston, 1977), p. 137.

107. As James Cargile has observed, the argument will not touch someone who holds "that one thing we can be sure of about the possible owner-operator of the universe is that he is the sort of being who will send religious people to heaven." ("Pascal's Wager," *Mind*, vol. 41 [1966], pp. 250–57 [see p. 253].) Or as another critic put it: "What Pascal overlooked was the hair-raising possibility that God might out-Luther Luther. . . . For God might punish those whose faith is prompted by prudence." Walter Kaufmann, *Critique of Religion and Philosophy* (New York, 1958), p. 122. It is not that Pascal "overlooked" this possibility, but rather that it does not square with the concept of God that Pascal held and that he himself took to share with those to whom his deliberations were addressed.

108. Antony Flew, "Is Pascal's Wager the Only Safe Bet?" *The Rationalist Annual*, vol. 76 (1960), pp. 21–25 (see pp. 24–25); reprinted in revised form in *God, Freedom, and Immortality* (Buffalo, 1984), pp. 61–68 (see pp. 66–67).

109. Michael Scriven, *Primary Philosophy* (New York, 1966), p. 151. Compare also:

> Again even if there were a god of Pascal's sort, there are various sub-possibilities to be taken into account: perhaps this god is not satisfied with mere belief in that there is *a* god, but adopts the principle *nulla salus extra ecclesiam,* where the church within which alone salvation is to be found is not necessarily the Church of Rome, but perhaps that of the Anabaptists or the Mormons or the Muslim Sunnis or the worshippers of Kali or of Odin. Who can say? From the position of initial ignorance and non-reliance on reason in which Pascal starts, no such possibility is more likely than any other. (J. L. Mackie, *The Miracle of Theism* [Oxford, 1982], p. 203.)

One of the curious features of the literature on Pascal's Wager is that even his otherwise conscientious critics repeat the same old counter-arguments without ever acknowledging the contributions of their predecessors.

110. Thus when one recent writer objects against a critic of Pascal that "it is not obvious that there are an infinite number of (genuinely) possible supernatural beings," he speaks, if not the truth, then at any rate the view most people take of the matter. (Michel Martin, "On Four Critiques of Pascal's Wager," *Sophia,* vol. 14 [1975], pp. 1–11 [see p. 10].) Most people have enough difficulty with the traditional idea of God without fretting about an endless proliferation of conceivable alternatives.

111. Cf. Antony Flew, *God and Philosophy* (London, 1966), sect. 9.15. Compare: "Another possibility is that there might be a god who looked with more favor on honest doubters and atheists who, in Hume's words, proportioned their belief to the evidence, than on mercinary manipulators of their own understanding." (John Mackie, *The Miracle of Theism* [Oxford, 1982], p. 203.)

112. George Schlesinger, *Religion and Scientific Method* (Dordrecht and Boston, 1977), p. 137.

113. Daniel Huet as quoted in M. J. Oeuvre, "Le Fragment infinirien et ses sources" in *Blaise Pascal: l'Homme et l'oeuvre,* Cahiers de Royaumont, Philosophie I (Paris, 1956), pp. 159–86 (see p. 183, n. 89).

114. *Pensées,* 214/282.

115. Some of the issues that would arise here are discussed in Herbert Fingarette, *Self-Deception* (New York, 1969).

116. William James, *The Will to Believe* (New York and London, 1896), pp. 24–25.

117. For a good account of the Prisoner's Dilemma see Morton D. David, *Game Theory* (New York, 1970), pp. 92–103. See also A. Rapoport and A. M. Chammah, *Prisoner's Dilemma: A Study in Conflict and Cooperation* (Ann Arbor, 1965), and Anatol Rapoport, "Escape from Paradox," *American Scientist,* vol. 217 (1967), pp. 50–56.

118. "For the virtues are naturally linked to living pleasurably, and living pleasurably is inseparable from them." Epicurus, *Letter to Menoeceus,* 132.

119. Compare Hans Küng's stress on our fundamental commitment to "a trust in which I stake myself without security or guarantee . . . for either I regard reality . . . as trustworthy and reliable—or not." (*Does God Exist?* [London, 1980; tr. from the German *Existiert Gott?,* Munich, 1978], p. 438.) Küng explicitly compares his situation with that of Pascal's Wager.

120. The analogy between Pascal's argumentation and one recent legitimation of moral principles (viz., that of John Rawls) is drawn in chap. 7, "Rawls and Pascal's Wager," of Bernard Williams' *Moral Luck* (Cambridge, 1981), pp. 94–100. As Rawls sees it, the contractarian moralist contemplates a choice under uncertainty regarding the fortuitous contingencies of matters in this world. Pascal, on the other hand, contemplates choice under uncertainty regarding the inherently unpredictable conditions of a (possible) world to come.

121. See Douglas R. Hofstader in *Scientific American,* vol. 248 (May, 1983), pp. 16–26, regarding the case for trust and cooperation even in a world of self-interested agents.

122. For an interesting recent discussion of the theological ramifications of hope see J. L. Muyskens, *The Sufficiency of Hope: The Conceptual Foundations of Religion* (Philadelphia, 1979).

123. Immanuel Kant, *Religion Within the Limits of Reason Alone,* tr. T. M. Greene and H. H. Hudson (Chicago, 1934), p. 173.

IV. Is a Practically Grounded Faith Unworthy?

124. Paul Levy, *Moore* (New York, 1979), p. 214.

125. Compare John King-Farlow, "Lachelier's Idealism," *Idealistic Studies,* vol. 12 (1982), pp. 72–78 (see pp. 75-76). As Pascal says about faith toward the end of the *infini-rien* passage: "I tell you, you will thereby profit in this life." (*Pensées,* 343/233, *ad fin.*) But

this consideration plays no role in the argument. It is an incidental side benefit, not a probatively relevant consideration.

126. See William James, *The Will to Believe and Other Essays in Popular Philosophy* (New York, 1896).

127. Ibid., pp. 5–6.

128. Ibid.

129. *Pensées,* 575/283.

130. *Pensées,* 225/278.

131. *Pensées,* 224/277.

Name Index

Subject Index